Improving Reading Comprehension with 20 Key Reading Skills

READING CATCH

Kirsty Taylor

Contents

Introduction

Introducing Reading Catch

Reading Catch contains 20 interesting passages on a diverse range of topics. With each passage, students will learn 20 key reading comprehension skills vital to the proper usage of the English language. They will complete exercises centered upon reading skills, and build a firm understanding of the reading skills outlined in American education standards.

Pre-reading

- **Skill Introduction** gives students detailed information about the target reading skill. - - - - - - - - -
- **Warm-up Question** - - - - - - - - - - - - - - -

Reading

- **Before you read** - - - - - - - - - -
- **Word definitions** - - - - - - - - - -
- **Passage** with vivid illustrations is interesting to young students. The target reading skill is applied in context that makes the reading relevant. - - - - - - - - - -

After reading

- **Vocabulary Exercise** - - - - - - - -
- **Comprehension Questions**
- **Focus on Skill** offers students various questions focused on the target reading skill. - - - - - - - -

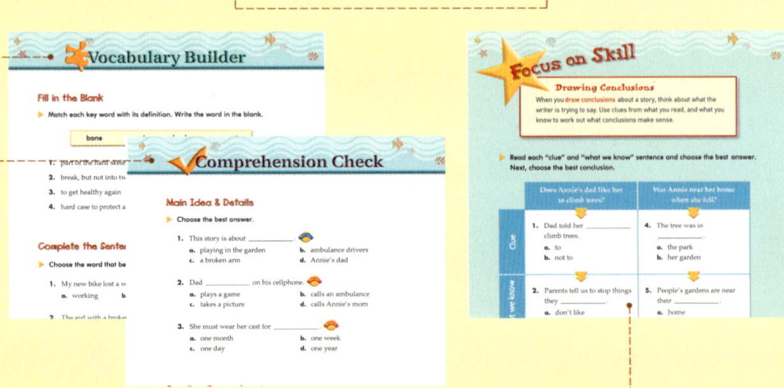

Drawing Conclusions

READING SKILL

When you read a story, you may need to think about what the author doesn't tell you.

Clue
Clue → Conclusion

Skill Strategy Use the words and pictures as clues. Then think about what you already know.

▶ **Read the story. Draw conclusions about what happens.**

Most kids walk to school every day, but Andrew could not walk. He went everywhere in his wheelchair. He didn't need anyone to push him because he had an electric chair.

   Andrew was scared on the first day of middle school. The other boys might laugh at him because he was the only boy with a wheelchair.

   The other boys were running and playing football. Andrew was worried. When he got to the school yard, the other boys came over to look at his chair. "Wow, cool!" one boy said. "Your wheelchair is amazing! I want one too!"

Choose the correct answer to complete the sentences below.

1. Andrew ______________ play football with the other boys.

   a. can   **b.** cannot

2. The other boys ______________ Andrew's wheelchair.

   a. don't like   **b.** like

DRAWING CONCLUSIONS
Language Arts

Before you read

1. Have you ever broken a bone?
2. How can you help a broken bone heal quickly?

VOCABULARY

broken adj.
smashed in pieces

ambulance n.
a vehicle that takes people who are sick or hurt to a hospital.

emergency room n.
place in a hospital for treating people who need help quickly

x-ray n.
a special kind of photo that shows the bones inside the body

broken

Annie loved climbing trees. She could climb higher than anyone else she knew. She climbed them even when her dad told her to stop, but one day she got a nasty surprise. She climbed the tallest tree in her garden. She got to the top then "snap!" the branch was **broken**. Annie fell to the ground!

"Ouch!" shouted Annie. "Help me!"

Her dad heard her shouting, so he came running out of the house. He called an **ambulance** on his cellphone.

"I told you not to climb trees!" said Dad.

Annie's arm hurt a lot. She was worried that it might be broken.

The ambulance came very quickly and took Annie to hospital. She had to go to the **emergency room**.

The doctor gave her an **x-ray**. He showed Annie the x-ray picture of her arm. She could see her **bone** with a long black line on it.

"You have **cracked** your bone." the doctor said, after he had looked at her arm.

"You will need to get a **cast**. You should wear it for a month so that your arm can **heal**."

"Oh!" said Annie. "If I have a cast on my arm, I can't climb any trees anymore!"

"Good!" said Dad.

bone n.
part of the hard skeleton inside the body

crack v.
to break, but not into two pieces

cast n.
a hard case to protect a broken bone

heal v.
to get healthy again

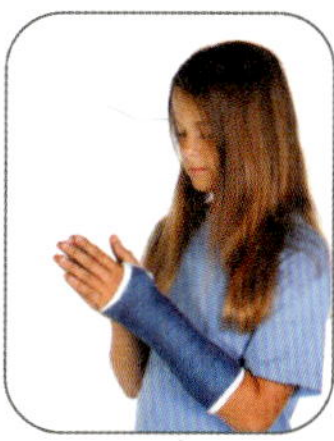

cast

Vocabulary Builder

Fill in the Blank

▶ **Match each key word with its definition. Write the word in the blank.**

bone	crack	heal	cast

1. part of the hard skeleton inside the body   ___________

2. break, but not into two pieces   ___________

3. to get healthy again   ___________

4. hard case to protect a broken bone   ___________

Complete the Sentence

▶ **Choose the word that best completes the sentence.**

1. My new bike lost a wheel. It is ___________.

    a. working   **b.** broken   **c.** great   **d.** fast

2. The girl with a broken arm had to go to the ___________.

    a. visitor's room   **b.** dining room   **c.** TV room   **d.** emergency room

3. A(n) ___________ picture shows you the inside of things.

    a. color   **b.** x-ray   **c.** large   **d.** cast

4. If someone needs to go to hospital you should call a(n) ___________.

    a. ambulance   **b.** fire engine   **c.** police car   **d.** teacher

Comprehension Check

Main Idea & Details

▶ **Choose the best answer.**

1. This story is about ______________. *Main Idea*
- **a.** playing in the garden
- **b.** ambulance drivers
- **c.** a broken arm
- **d.** Annie's dad

2. Dad ______________ on his cellphone. *Details*
- **a.** plays a game
- **b.** calls an ambulance
- **c.** takes a picture
- **d.** calls Annie's mom

3. She must wear her cast for ______________. *Details*
- **a.** one month
- **b.** one week
- **c.** one day
- **d.** one year

Reading Comprehension

▶ **Circle T for true or F for false.**

1. Annie's dad thinks it is a good idea to climb trees.   T   F

2. The ambulance takes a long time to arrive.   T   F

3. Annie can climb trees with her cast on.   T   F

Focus on Skill

Drawing Conclusions

When you **draw conclusions** about a story, think about what the writer is trying to say. Use clues from what you read, and what you know to work out what conclusions make sense.

▶ **Read each "clue" and "what we know" sentence and choose the best answer. Next, choose the best conclusion.**

	Does Annie's dad like her to climb trees?	Was Annie near her home when she fell?
Clue	**1.** Dad told her __________ climb trees. **a.** to **b.** not to	**4.** The tree was in __________. **a.** the park **b.** her garden
What we know	**2.** Parents tell us to stop things they __________. **a.** don't like **b.** like	**5.** People's gardens are near their __________. **a.** home **b.** school
Conclusion	**3.** Annie's dad __________ like her to climb trees. **a.** does **b.** doesn't	**6.** Annie was __________. **a.** near home **b.** far from home

Sequencing: Order of Events

READING SKILL

Knowing the order of events will help you understand the story better.

Event 1 → Event 2 → Event 3

Signal Words *first, next, then, finally, last, before, after*

▶ **Read the story about a little puppy.**

I went grocery shopping at 11am. Mr. Piggles stayed home. I walked into the kitchen two hours later.

First, I stepped on Mr Piggles' toy. *Next*, my grocery bag fell out of my hand, and the eggs broke. *Then*, I walked into the living room. There was newspaper everywhere. *Finally*, I found Mr. Piggles in my bedroom. He was chewing on my shoes. Bad Mr. Piggles!

Write the numbers in the blanks to show the order of events.

_______ I saw newspaper all over the living room.

_______ I dropped eggs onto the kitchen floor.

_______ I found the puppy eating my shoes.

_______ I left the house to buy food and drinks.

_______ I stepped on a toy in the kitchen.

Before you read

1. What kinds of birthday presents do you like?
2. What kinds of animals do people like as pets?

VOCABULARY

share v.
to use or enjoy something together

attic n.
space in a house directly under the roof

bark v.
(of dogs) to make a loud noise

turn n.
opportunity to do something in a certain order

share

Happy Birthday

Mr. Valentine was in his kitchen baking a birthday cake for his wife. She loved banana cake. Mrs. Valentine was also in the kitchen. She was baking a birthday cake, too. It was for her husband. He loved apple cake. Mr. and Mrs. Valentine **shared** the same birthday!

First, Mr. Valentine said: "I want to give you your birthday present." He went to the **attic** and came back with a box. Mrs. Valentine laughed. The box was **barking**.

Next, Mrs. Valentine said, "Now it's my **turn**. I'll be right back." She walked to the **cellar** and came back with a box. Mr. Valentine laughed. Her box was barking, too.

Mr. and Mrs. Valentine had each **received** a puppy for their birthday! Mr. Valentine named his *Banana*, and Mrs. Valentine called hers *Apple*.

Then Mr. Valentine took Banana for a walk. Mrs. Valentine and Apple went into the kitchen to **decorate** the cakes. Ten minutes later Mr. Valentine and Banana **rushed** home. It was raining! There was only one thing to do. Finally they would eat the birthday cakes! Mr. Valentine and Banana ate apple cake loudly while Mrs. Valentine and Apple quietly ate banana cake.

Vocabulary Builder

Fill in the Blank

▶ **Match each key word with its definition. Write the word in the blank.**

receive	rush	cellar	attic

1. to act or go really quickly   _________________

2. room built under a house or building   _________________

3. to get or take   _________________

4. space in a house directly under the roof   _________________

Complete the Sentence

▶ **Choose the word that best completes the sentence.**

1. People _____________ sandwiches when they have a picnic.

    a. turn   **b.** write   **c.** read   **d.** share

2. Dogs _____________ when they get excited.

    a. read   **b.** turn   **c.** share   **d.** bark

3. We can _____________ Christmas trees with colored lights.

    a. turn   **b.** decorate   **c.** share   **d.** read

4. The children took _____________ playing on the slide at the park.

    a. barks   **b.** paints   **c.** turns   **d.** shares

Comprehension Check

Main Idea & Details

▶ **Choose the best answer.**

1. This story is about _____________ . 
- **a.** Christmas Day
- **b.** Valentine's Day
- **c.** a shared birthday
- **d.** a cake bakery

2. Mr. Valentine hid his wife's birthday present in the _____________ .
- **a.** attic
- **b.** kitchen
- **c.** cellar
- **d.** bedroom

3. Mrs. Valentine _____________ before she ate her birthday cake.
- **a.** walked her puppy
- **b.** cooked in the kitchen
- **c.** signed a birthday card
- **d.** decorated both cakes

Reading Comprehension

▶ **Circle T for true or F for false.**

1. Mr. Valentine decorated the birthday cakes and then walked the puppies. T F

2. Mrs. Valentine knew that her husband would give her a puppy. T F

3. Mr. Valentine shared his birthday cake with his puppy Banana. T F

Focus on Skill

Sequencing: Order of Events

When you know the order of events, you can understand and remember a story better. Use clue words, such as **first**, **next**, **then**, **last**, and **finally** to help you.

▶ **Read the question. Choose the correct answer.**

What happened after the cakes began to bake and before Mr. Valentine walked Banana?

a. Apple and Banana barked at each other and ran around the house.

b. The Valentines gave each other presents and named the puppies.

c. Apple helped Mrs. Valentine decorate both of the birthday cakes.

d. The Valentines gave their puppies names and ate cake together.

▶ **What happened in the story? Number the events to show story order.**

_______ Mr. Valentine walked Banana.

_______ Mr. and Mrs. Valentine baked birthday cakes together.

_______ Mrs. Valentine went to the cellar.

_______ Mr. and Mrs. Valentine exchanged birthday presents.

_______ Mrs. Valentine decorated the cakes.

_______ Mr. Valentine went to the attic.

_______ Mr. and Mrs. Valentine shared cake with their puppies.

_______ Mr. and Mrs. Valentine named their puppies.

Sequencing: Steps in a Process

READING SKILL

When you read about how to do something, think about the order of steps to take.

Step 1 → Step 2 → Step 3

Signal Words *first, next, then, finally, last, second, third, fourth*

▶ **Read the steps telling how to make a dancing ghost.**

You can make your own "dancing ghost." *First,* find some tissue paper and scissors. *Next,* cut out a ghost. Make it about 4cm long. *Then,* blow up a balloon and tie it. Quickly rub the balloon on your hair for ten seconds. *Last,* bring the balloon near the ghost.
Finally watch your ghost dance!

How do you make a dancing ghost? Number the steps to show the order.

_______ Bring the balloon close to the ghost.

_______ Make a ghost out of tissue paper.

_______ Rub the balloon through your hair.

_______ Blow up a balloon and tie it.

_______ Get tissue paper and a pair of scissors.

Before you read

1. Have you ever made a paper airplane?
2. Why do paper airplanes fly?

VOCABULARY

contest n.
game or race that people try to win

stay v.
to spend time in a place

ground n.
land

throw v.
to send through the air using your arm

ground

Hoop Glider

Paper airplanes are fun to make. Sometimes people have **contests** with them. They make planes, then throw them to see how far they can fly.

Some people make planes with shorter wings. They can fly high into the air, but they don't **stay** there. They quickly fall to the **ground**. Some people make planes with longer wings. They are hard to **throw** up high, but they stay in the air for longer. They are good at **gliding**. Some people make **Hoop gliders**. Hoop gliders can fly farther, and maybe win in a contest!

To make a hoop glider, you need four things: scissors, tape, an index card, and a plastic straw. When you have these things together, you are ready to start.

First, cut the card into three pieces. Make each piece the same size. Next, tape two pieces together to make a big hoop. **Overlap** them to make the hoop strong. The first piece will cover some of the second. Then, make a small hoop with the last piece. After that, tape the straw to the hoops. Put the straw on the inside! Then, pick up the straw. The hoops should be on top. Now throw your hoop glider into the air! Finally, you can see how far it flies.

hoop

Fill in the Blank

▶ **Match each key word with its definition. Write the word in the blank.**

overlap	stay	hoop	glide

1. to lie on top of something and cover   ________________

2. circle with a hole in the middle   ________________

3. to move softly through the air; float   ________________

4. to spend time in a place   ________________

Complete the Sentence

▶ **Choose the word that best completes the sentence.**

1. The children were sitting on the ____________ under the tree.
    a. plate   **b.** cat   **c.** hoop   **d.** ground

2. The ____________ flew gently through the air.
    a. monkey   **b.** glider   **c.** flower   **d.** chair

3. If you can ____________ well you might be good at basketball.
    a. overlap   **b.** glide   **c.** throw   **d.** eat

4. Tony won the hotdog eating ____________ by eating 15 hotdogs.
    a. run   **b.** team   **c.** contest   **d.** hoop

Comprehension Check

Main Idea & Details

▶ **Choose the best answer.**

1. This passage is about _____________. 
    a. how to make hoop gliders   **b.** why paper airplanes can fly
    c. how to use index cards   **d.** how to make paper hoops

2. What should you do before you make the small hoop?
    a. Glue the bigger hoop to the straw.
    b. Tape two pieces of index card together.
    c. Tape the bigger hoop to the straw.
    d. Cut the index card into three pieces.

3. Shorter-winged planes are easy to throw into the air, _____________. 
    a. and they are good at floating   **b.** but they will fly in circles
    c. but they are bad gliders   **d.** and they are good at flying.

Reading Comprehension

▶ **Circle T for true or F for false.**

1. Paper airplanes with longer wings are difficult to throw into the air.   **T**   **F**

2. Each piece cut from the index card is a different size.   **T**   **F**

3. You must throw the hoop glider into the air with the hoops on the bottom.   **T**   **F**

Sequence: Steps in a Process

When you read about how to do something, think about the order of steps. Clue words like **first**, **next**, **then**, and **finally** can help you understand the order in which things should be done.

▶ **How do you make a hoop glider? Number the steps to show the correct order.**

_______ Cut the index card into three pieces.

_______ Make a small hoop.

_______ Throw the hoop glider into the air.

_______ Find the things you need to make a hoop glider.

_______ Tape the straw to the inside of the hoops.

_______ Tape two pieces of index card together.

▶ **Match the clue word in the box to the correct step.**

Finally	Next	First

You have scissors, tape, an index card, and a drinking straw.

__________, cut the index card into three pieces.

__________, tape two pieces of the index card together.

Then, make a small hoop.

And then, tape the straw to the inside of the hoop.

__________, throw the hoop glider into the air.

LESSON 4 — Predicting Outcomes

READING SKILL

Sometimes you have to make a prediction about what happens next. Clues can help you.

Clue → Prediction

Skill Strategy Think about what the characters know, say and do.

▶ **Read the story.**

"I don't like milk, Mom," said Harry.

"Milk makes your teeth and bones hard," said Harry's mother.

"It helps you grow tall."

"But I don't like milk. And I want to play with my friends now."

"Eat first, play later," said Harry's mother. Then she smiled.

"You can have cheese instead of milk."

"I love cheese!" said Harry. "Thanks, Mom!"

What do you think will happen next? Choose the correct answer.

Harry will ______________ .

a. drink his milk	**b.** eat some cheese
c. play with his friends	**d.** eat some fish

PREDICTING OUTCOMES
Science

Before you read

1. What kinds of food do you like to eat?
2. What kinds of food are good for you?

favorite adj.
liked more than all others

nutritious adj.
having a lot of things that are good for the body

food pyramid n.
a picture showing the amount of different foods to eat every day

serving n.
the normal size of food or drink a person has

Healthy Eating

Mr. Bourne is very happy because today is his birthday. Today is also his **favorite** day of the school year. He gets to teach his students about eating **nutritious** food.

Mr. Bourne started to draw a **food pyramid** for his students. It would show them what to eat every day and how much. First he would say, "Eat six **servings** from the **grain** group every day. Grain foods like rice and bread give you **energy**." Next he would tell them, "Eat four servings of **colorful** fruits and vegetables each day. Red peppers, orange carrots, green spinach, and blue blueberries help your body."

Then he would say, "Drink three glasses of milk every day. Or eat yogurt or cheese. They make your bones and teeth strong." Finally he would tell them, "Eat two servings of meat or beans each day for strong muscles."

Mr. Bourne looked at the last food group on the food pyramid: fats and **sweets**. Then Mr. Bourne looked at the chocolate cake. He knew fats and sweets were not healthy, but he also knew his 15 students liked cake a lot. He said, "Cake does taste good! A little fat and sugar every day is okay." He cut the cake into 15 pieces and waited for his students to arrive.

colorful

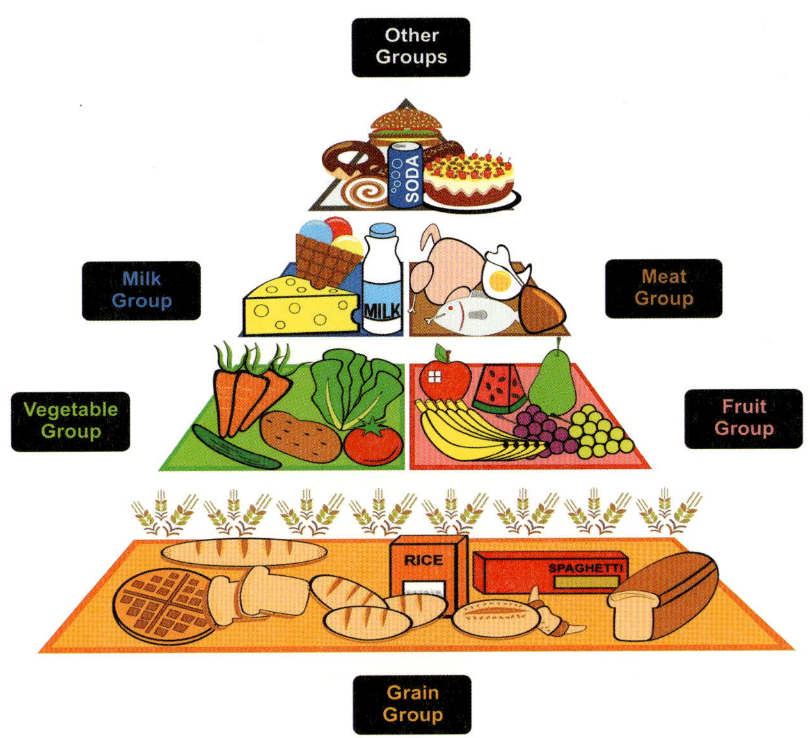

Vocabulary Builder

Fill in the Blank

▶ **Match each key word with its definition. Write the word in the blank.**

| serving   grain   nutritious   food pyramid |

1. dried food such as wheat, corn, or rice ___________________

2. a picture showing the amount of different foods to eat every day ___________________

3. size of food or drink a person normally has ___________________

4. having a lot of things that are good for the body ___________________

Complete the Sentence

▶ **Choose the word that best completes the sentence.**

1. I like Italian restaurants because pizza is my _______________ food.

   a. worst   **b.** favorite   **c.** healthy   **d.** green

2. Eating _______________ is bad for your teeth.

   a. sweets   **b.** salad   **c.** rice   **d.** meat

3. You need a lot of _______________ if you want to run fast.

   a. sunshine   **b.** chocolate   **c.** energy   **d.** clothes

4. A rainbow is very _______________ .

   a. dull   **b.** colorful   **c.** heavy   **d.** dark

Main Idea & Details

▶ **Choose the best answer.**

1. This story is about _______________ . Main Idea

   a. fast food   **b.** making a birthday cake

   c. how to eat healthily   **d.** Mr. Bourne's birthday party

2. People should eat _______________ servings of fruit and vegetables Details
every day.

   a. two   **b.** three

   c. four   **d.** six

3. Muscles need _______________ to grow strong. Details

   a. milk and cheese   **b.** meat and beans

   c. rice and bread   **d.** peppers and carrots

Reading Comprehension

▶ **Circle T for true or F for false.**

1. Sweets are good for your teeth .   **T**   **F**

2. Teeth and bones need milk and cheese to become hard.   **T**   **F**

3. Fats and sweets should never be eaten.   **T**   **F**

Predicting Outcomes

Predict what might happen next in a story. Think about what the characters know, say, and do. Then think about what you know to figure things out.

▶ **Read the sentence, then make a prediction.**

1. Mr. Bourne drew a food pyramid.

Mr. Bourne will _____________ .

   a. let the students draw too

   b. teach a math class

   c. teach about nutrition

   d. give the students cake

2. The students must learn about unhealthy fats and sweets.

Mr. Bourne will _____________ .

   a. tell students to eat a lot of fatty foods

   b. warn students about unhealthy foods

   c. tell students sweets are good for their health

   d. warn students about eating too much fruit

3. Mr. Bourne cut the cake into 15 pieces.

Mr. Bourne will _____________ .

   a. eat 15 pieces of cake himself

   b. tell the students not to eat cake

   c. give one student 15 pieces of cake

   d. give each student a piece of cake

LESSON 5 Cause and Effect

READING SKILL

In a story, some events make other things happen. **Causes** make things happen. The things thathappen are **effects**.

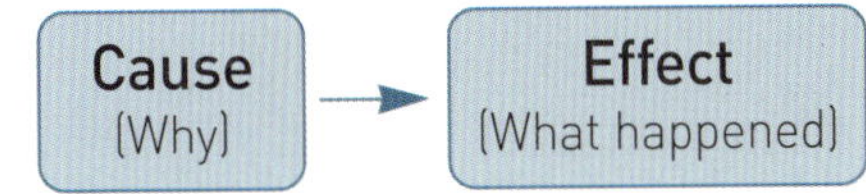

Signal Words *because, since, so, therefore, as a result*

▶ **Read the article, then match the correct effect to each cause below.**

Many people drive cars to get to work every day *because* they want to travel quickly. When lots of people drive cars the roads are very busy *so* traffic moves very slowly and people cannot get to work as quickly as they would like!

Since bicycles take up less space on roads and buses can carry a lot of people at one time, using more bicycles and buses can lead to quieter and faster roads.

Cause	Effect
1. Many people drive cars to get to work every day.	**a.** The roads will be busy and traffic will move quickly.
	b. The roads will be busy and traffic will move slowly.
2. Many people use buses and bicycles to get to work everyday.	**c.** The roads will be less busy and traffic will move quickly.
	d. The roads will be less busy and traffic will move slowly.

Before you read

1. What do we use energy for?
2. Where can we get energy from?

VOCABULARY

energy n.
a source of usable power

source n.
where something comes from

oil n.
a liquid found under the ground that can power machines

gasoline n.
a liquid burned in many cars' engines as fuel

oil

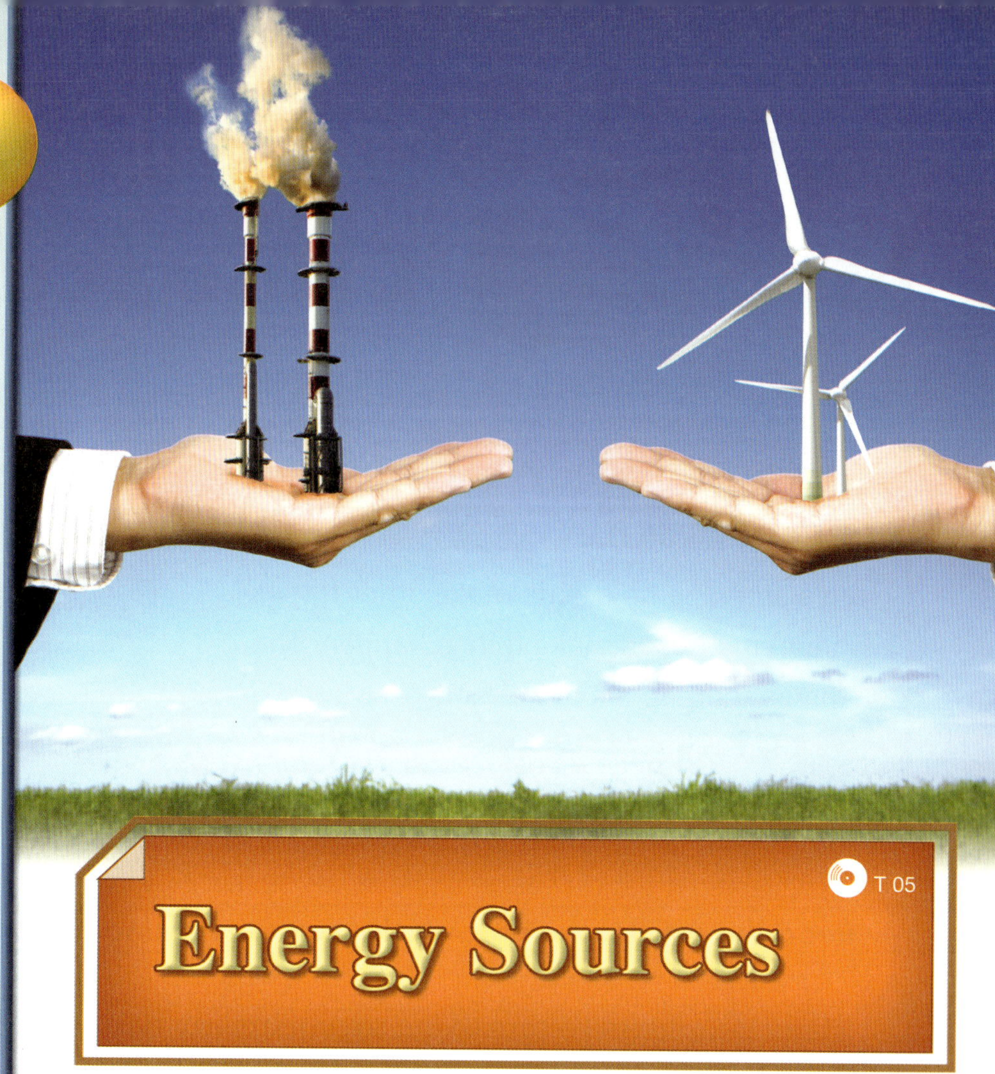

T 05

Energy Sources

We need energy to make things work. Without **energy**, we wouldn't have computers, TVs or cellphones. But where does energy come from? Right now, the world's main energy **source** is **oil**. We get 35% of our energy from oil, which comes from under the ground or under the sea.

Some oil is turned into **gasoline**, then used to make cars and trucks work. We can also have **electricity** to use as energy in our homes, schools and offices because of oil burned in power stations.

Oil is an important energy source but there are many problems with oil. It is a dirty energy source. So burning it can cause **pollution** in our air and therefore people can get sick from the dirty air. There is also a **limited** amount of oil. One day there will be no oil left. We must find other energy sources to use. We can get energy using the water, sun and wind.

The wind, sun and water will always be there and they do not cause pollution, so it is a good idea to get energy from them. At the moment, the world gets just 6% of energy from water, and less than 2% from sun and wind together. **Scientists** are trying to find ways to get more energy from these sources, since if they do we will always have enough clean energy!

pollution

Vocabulary Builder

Fill in the Blank

▶ **Match each key word with its definition. Write the word in the blank.**

limited	oil	electricity	gasoline

1. a liquid burned in many cars' engines as fuel _______________

2. having a certain amount and no more _______________

3. a kind of energy used to make lights and other things work _______________

4. a liquid found under the ground that can power machines _______________

Complete the Sentence

▶ **Choose the word that best completes the sentence.**

1. The lake's water was dirty because of the _______________ from the factory.
   a. sun   **b.** wind   **c.** pollution   **d.** electricity

2. Turn off the lights in your home if you want to save more _______________ .
   a. energy   **b.** paper   **c.** food   **d.** time

3. The river's _______________ started high in the mountains.
   a. hair   **b.** end   **c.** dry   **d.** source

4. _______________ study to learn about the world around us.
   a. Pollutions   **b.** Scientists   **c.** Sources   **d.** Drivers

Comprehension Check

Main Idea & Details

▶ **Choose the best answer.**

1. This story is about ______________. 
   - **a.** clean and dirty energy
   - **b.** dirty air
   - **c.** using solar power
   - **d.** the price of gasoline

2. ______________ is not a source of energy.
   - **a.** The wind
   - **b.** Oil
   - **c.** A computer
   - **d.** The sun

3. Oil is found ______________.
   - **a.** in rainwater
   - **b.** under the ground
   - **c.** above the sun
   - **d.** in electricity

Reading Comprehension

▶ **Circle T for true or F for false.**

1. We will always have oil.　　T　F

2. Oil is the world's only energy source.　　T　F

3. We can use wind as an energy source.　　T　F

Focus on Skill

Cause and Effect

When reading, think about what happens and why. Clue words such as **because**, **since**, **so** and **therefore** can help you.

▶ **Choose the correct answers.**

Cause	Clue word	Effect

1. The sun and wind will ____________ .
  a. never be there **b.** always be there
  c. always be away **d.** run out one day
 	
2. The ____________ pollution.
  a. always cause **b.** sometimes cause
  c. might cause **d.** do not cause
	so	It is a good idea to get energy from them.

Cause	Clue word	Effect

Oil is a dirty energy source.	so
	
	therefore
		3. Burning it can cause ____________ .
		  a. pollution **b.** energy
		  c. electricity **d.** gasoline
		
		4. People can ____________ .
		  a. drive their cars a lot
		  b. use their computers a lot
		  c. get sick from dirty air
		  d. buy a lot of gasoline

Real and Make-believe

READING SKILL

Real stories can happen in real life.
Make-believe stories can never actually happen.

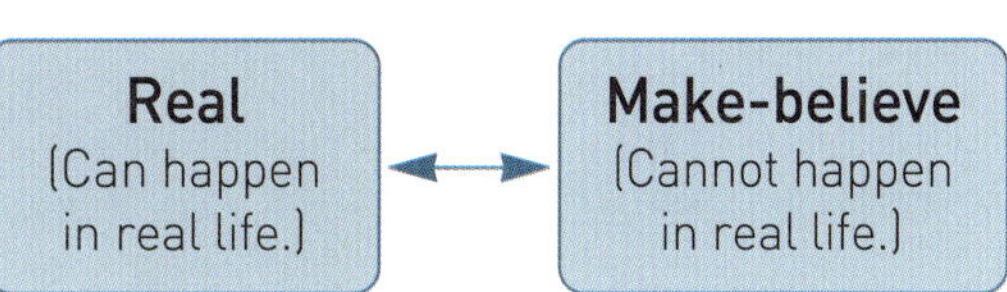

Skill Strategy In make-believe stories, animals and objects might talk and people could do magic.

▶ **Read both stories. Then answer the questions.**

A. Keiko was excited. She was going to pick out a new piano today. The last one Keiko saw was her favorite. It was checkered bright purple and black. It was perfect.

B. "I wonder if she is a good pianist." Keiko's piano said to its stool. "I don't know." said the stool, "but I hope Keiko likes to practice every day."

Circle the correct answer.

1. Which story is realistic?

    a. A   **b.** B

2. Which story is make-believe?

    a. A   **b.** B

**REAL AND
MAKE-BELIEVE**
Art

Before you read

1. Do you enjoy real life or make-believe stories more?

2. What would you do in a make-believe world?

VOCABULARY

conductor n.
a person who directs an orchestra

orchestra n.
a large group of musicians who play together

section n.
one of several parts that go together to form a whole

string n.
musical instruments that have strings

conductor

The Conductor

Mozi was a **conductor**. His job was to help the musicians in the **orchestra** play well together. He waved his arms up and down, left and right counting out the time. He moved his hands through the air to show the musicians when to play softly or loudly.

Today Mozi is tired. He and the orchestra have been working hard for their big concert. Mozi was worried — what if the musicians make a mistake?

The four **sections** of the orchestra hadn't arrived yet. No **strings**, **woodwinds**, **brass**, or **percussion** musicians. The room was very quiet so Mozi closed his eyes.

Suddenly, the whole orchestra was in front of

him.

"Are you musicians ready? It is time for our big concert. The **audience** is listening to every sound we make."

Then Mozi saw the musicians were not there — the instruments were playing themselves!

The brass section blew, "You strings always sit at the front. It's our turn! Move over, violins!" they said.

The percussion section's drums yelled, "You woodwinds are too quiet. Get out of the orchestra!"

The music sounded terrible. What was he going to do!

"Mozi? Mozi!" someone said. "Wake up! The musicians are here."

Vocabulary Builder

Fill in the Blank

▶ **Match each key word with its definition. Write the word in the blank.**

| string | audience | section | conductor |

1. musical instruments that have strings   ________________

2. a person who directs an orchestra   ________________

3. people who have come together to listen or watch   ________________

4. one of several parts   ________________

Complete the Sentence

▶ **Choose the word that best completes the sentence.**

1. She played the drums in the ____________ section of the band.
   a. string   **b.** brass   **c.** percussion   **d.** woodwind

2. The trumpet is a(n) ____________ instrument.
   a. string   **b.** brass   **c.** section   **d.** audience

3. The ____________ had woodwind, string, brass and percussion sections.
   a. brass band   **b.** rock band   **c.** drum group   **d.** orchestra

4. You play ____________ instruments by blowing into them.
   a. audience   **b.** woodwind   **c.** percussion   **d.** string

Comprehension Check

Main Idea & Details

▶ **Choose the best answer.**

1. The article is about a(n) _____________ . 
   - **a.** argument in an orchestra
   - **b.** orchestra that doesn't practice
   - **c.** terrible concert
   - **d.** worried conductor's dream

2. A conductor's job is to help musicians _____________ .
   - **a.** play music together well
   - **b.** play as loudly as they want
   - **c.** sit in the correct orchestra section
   - **d.** write their own music

3. Mozi the conductor dreamed that the _____________ .
   - **a.** brass section attacked him
   - **b.** musical instruments were arguing
   - **c.** musicians in his orchestra didn't show up
   - **d.** orchestra made mistakes and the audience left

Reading Comprehension

▶ **Circle T for true or F for false.**

1. The musicians had three more days until their concert.   T   F

2. Mozi was worried about how the concert would go.   T   F

3. The percussion section argued with the woodwind section.   T   F

Real and Make-believe

Some parts of stories could happen in real life — these events are **realistic**. Other parts tell about things that could never happen in real life — these are **make-believe**.

▶ **Choose the correct answer.**

What part of the story is make-believe?

a. Mozi waiting for the musicians
b. Mozi worrying about the concert
c. What happens in Mozi's dream
d. Someone waking Mozi up

▶ **Read each story event. Tick the correct boxes.**

	Real	Make -believe
1. Mozi helped the musicians in the orchestra play their music well.		
2. Mozi used his arms and hands to tell the musicians how to play.		
3. Mozi was very tired.		
4. The brass instruments wanted the string instruments to move.		
5. The percussion instruments yelled, "You woodwinds are too quiet!"		

READING SKILL

Words or phrases that help you guess the meanings of new words are context clues.

Skill Strategy Read sentences around the new word. You might find words with the same or opposite meanings, or explanations to help you.

▶ **Read about Sarah's marathon training. Answer the questions to show the meaning of the new words.**

Sarah is a schoolteacher in the daytime but she does something different in the evenings. She is **training** to run a **marathon**. She has to practice a lot of running to get fit for the 42 kilometer race.

1. Training means to ______________ .

   a. do something different
   b. practice a lot
   c. run

2. A marathon is a ______________ .

   a. schoolteacher
   b. 42 kilometer race
   c. daytime

Before you read

1. Are you good at sports?
2. Do you think you could ever be an Ironman?

VOCABULARY

prefer v.
to like one thing better than another

break n.
a period of time when something stops

stamina n.
the strength to handle long effort

combine v.
to bring together into a whole

Ironman Contest

Have you ever been on a long bike ride? Maybe you **prefer** to go swimming. Maybe it is jogging you like best. Think about doing all these things. Can you imagine doing them with no **break**? People who do all these things well without stopping can call themselves the Ironman.

The Ironman contest began as an argument between some runners and a swimming team on the island of Hawaii, USA. Both groups said they had better **stamina** than the other. They thought they were strong enough to keep doing sports for longer. They decided to have a race

combining all these events to see who was right. They would put all the different sports together then see who did them best!

The first Hawaiian Ironman competition began on February 18th 1978. The rules were: "Swim 2.4 miles! Bike 112 miles! Run 26.2 miles! **Brag** for the rest of your life!" If they finished, people could tell others how great they were.

Twelve people **completed** the race, with Gordon Haller finishing first. In the next year, the first female competitor, Lyn Lemaire, finished 6th.

Although the most famous Ironman contest still takes place in Hawaii, there are **similar** events like it all over the world. They are very **popular** so many people train hard to enter.

Vocabulary Builder

Fill in the Blank

▶ **Match each key word with its definition. Write the word in the blank.**

| stamina | combine | popular | brag |

1. to speak proudly about something you do or have ___________________

2. to bring together into a whole ___________________

3. liked by many people ___________________

4. the strength to handle long effort ___________________

Complete the Sentence

▶ **Choose the word that best completes the sentence.**

1. The two sisters looked very _______________.

    a. similar   **b.** complete   **c.** difficult   **d.** sunny

2. I _______________ swimming to running.

    a. similar   **b.** complete   **c.** stamina   **d.** prefer

3. If you don't _______________ the exam you won't get a good mark.

    a. stamina   **b.** complete   **c.** brag   **d.** prefer

4. Lunch _______________ is my favorite part of the workday!

    a. popular   **b.** prefer   **c.** break   **d.** similar

✓ Comprehension Check

Main Idea & Details

▶ **Read the sentences below. Choose the best answer.**

1. The article is about a(n) ______________ .
   a. Ironman competition   b. swimming race
   c. cycle race   d. running competition

2. An Ironman competition puts different ______________ .
   a. prizes together   b. sports together
   c. prizes apart   d. sports apart

3. The first event was on the ______________ .
   a. town of Hawaii   b. city of the USA
   c. country of Hawaii   d. island of Hawaii

Reading Comprehension

▶ **Circle T for true or F for false.**

1. Competitors must swim 26 miles.   T   F

2. Twelve people competed in the first race.   T   F

3. Lyn Lemaire won the second race.   T   F

Context Clues

Try to find the meaning of new words by reading the sentences around them. Look for words that mean the same as or the opposite of the new word to help you.

▶ **Use context clues to complete the sentences, then say if the context clue had the same or opposite meaning of the new word.**

1. I _____________ cake to chips because I like sweet things best.

- **a.** dislike
- **b.** hate
- **c.** prefer
- **d.** want

Type of context clue:

- **a.** opposite
- **b.** same meaning

2. Our bags are not _____________. They are different colors.

- **a.** unalike
- **b.** similar
- **c.** colorful
- **d.** bright

Type of context clue:

- **a.** opposite
- **b.** same meaning

3. The TV show was not _____________. Everyone disliked it.

- **a.** popular
- **b.** unpopular
- **c.** hated
- **d.** boring

Type of context clue:

- **a.** opposite
- **b.** same meaning

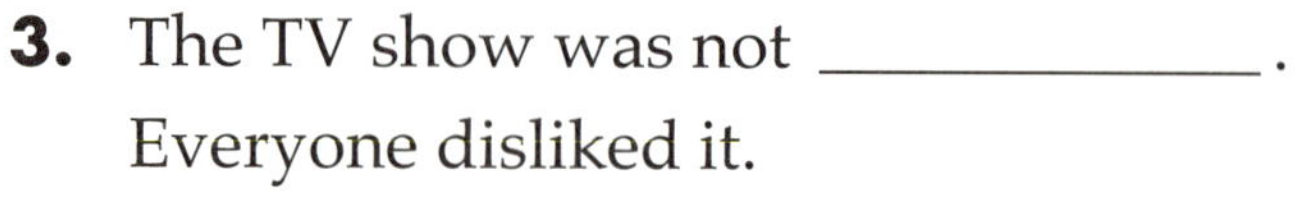

 Classifying

> **READING SKILL**
>
> You can **classify** things in a story into different groups. When things are the same in an important way, you can group them together.
>
> | Group 1 | Group 2 | Group 3 |
> | --- | --- | --- |
> | | | |
> | | | |
>
> Skill Strategy Think about what makes the things alike or different.

▶ **Read about Rachel's sports skills.**

Rachel was great at playing ball games. She was good at baseball, basketball and even soccer. She was very fit, but she was less good at running than ball games. She was no good at water sports however because she couldn't swim. She was also afraid of heights, so she would never be good at gliding either!

Which sports is Rachel good at? Write the correct letters in the correct group.

> **a.** gliding **b.** running **c.** baseball
> **d.** basketball **e.** swimming **f.** soccer

1. Sports Rachel is good at. _________________

2. Sports Rachel is less good at. _________________

3. Sports Rachel is bad at. _________________

feather

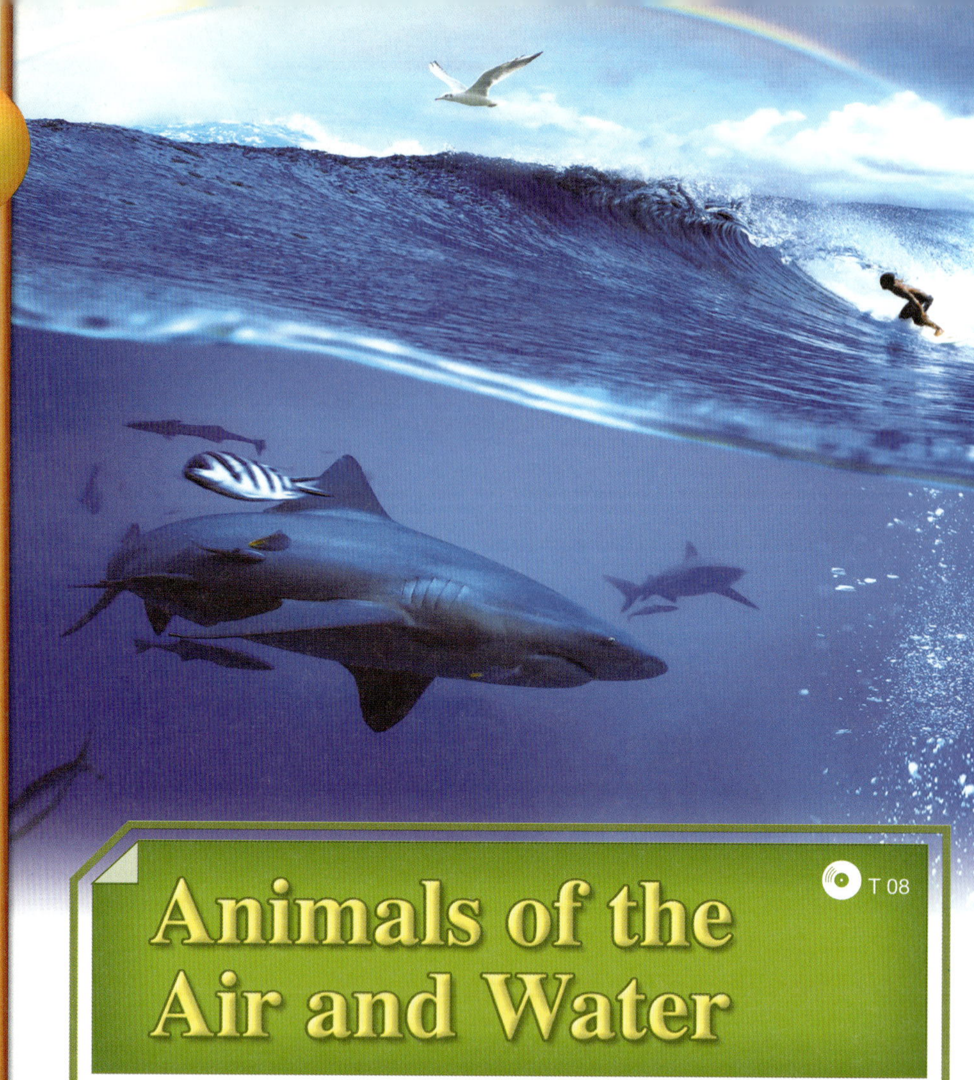

Animals of the Air and Water

T 08

Birds, fish and **insects** have very different bodies because they all need to do different things.

Most birds have very light bodies and **wings** covered with **feathers** to help them fly. Peregrine falcons have very thin wings, helping them to fly up to 320 kilometers an hour. They are the fastest flying birds on earth. Terns fly for longer than any other birds. They can stay in the air for up to ten years at a time, only landing to lay eggs.

Their **webbed** feet mean they can also swim, but they don't swim a lot.

Of course butterflies cannot swim, but their beautiful wings help them to fly well. Like many insects, their light bodies let them land on tiny twigs and leaves. Water beetles are insects that can fly and also swim. They carry an air bubble under their bodies to help them **breathe** when swimming.

Fish have bodies covered with **scales** and **gills** to breathe under water. Sharks are the biggest fish in the sea with large fins to help them swim. Flying fish can glide through the air using large **fins** that look like wings!

Although penguins have wings, they cannot fly through the air. These birds use their wings to glide through the water instead!

breathe v.
to take air in and out through the lungs

scale n.
one of many small, thin plates that cover fish

gill n.
an organ used by fish for breathing under water

fin n.
a thin, flat body part of fish used for swimming

gill

Fill in the Blank

▶ **Match each key word with its definition. Write the word in the blank.**

gill	scale	fin	wing

1. a thin, flat body part of fish used for swimming ___________________

2. an organ used by fish for breathing under water ___________________

3. a body part insects and birds use to fly ___________________

4. one of many small, thin plates that cover fish ___________________

Complete the Sentence

▶ **Choose the word that best completes the sentence.**

1. Birds have _____________ on their bodies but humans have skin.

    a. fur   **b.** scales   **c.** hair   **d.** feathers

2. Birds with _____________ feet can swim well.

    a. small   **b.** broken   **c.** webbed   **d.** clawed

3. Humans do not have gills so we cannot _____________ under water.

    a. breathe   **b.** see   **c.** swim   **d.** dive

4. A butterfly is a kind of _____________ but a penguin is not.

    a. bird   **b.** insect   **c.** fish   **d.** shark

Main Idea & Details

▶ **Read the sentences below. Choose the best answer.**

1. The story is about animals that ______________ . *Main Idea*
   - **a.** cannot fly
   - **b.** fly and swim
   - **c.** glide
   - **d.** cannot swim

2. Sharks are the ______________ in the sea. *Details*
   - **a.** smallest fish
   - **b.** best swimmers
   - **c.** biggest fish
   - **d.** best gliders

3. Terns can stay in the air for ______________ . *Details*
   - **a.** at least twelve years
   - **b.** for less than three years
   - **c.** for up to ten years
   - **d.** for more than ten years

Reading Comprehension

▶ **Circle T for true or F for false.**

1. Fish have feathers to help them swim.   T   F

2. Flying fish can glide through the air.   T   F

3. Penguins are good at flying.   T   F

Classifying

Classify things you read about to see how they are alike or different. Things that are similar should go together, and things that are different should go in separate groups.

▶ **Think about the different animals named in the article. Write the letters in the correct group to classify them.**

a. peregrine falcon   **b.** penguin

c. tern   **d.** water beetle

e. flying fish   **f.** butterfly

g. shark

1. Can fly

2. Can fly and swim

3. Can swim

Summarizing

READING SKILL

Summarizing is telling the most important part of a passage. It should give the main ideas but leave out details that are not important.

Skill Strategy Asking questions about *who*, *what*, *when* and *where* can help you find the main ideas to include in the summary.

▶ **Read the article. Choose the sentences that tells the main points in a shorter way.**

There are many kinds of homes. Apartments are good for cities while farmhouses are best for the country. In very rainy places you sometimes find stilt houses. Wooden posts lift the houses up high. Too much rain can cause floods but people who live in stilt houses don't worry. They stay high and dry!

a. There are many homes in cities and countries. Wooden posts lift houses and people don't need to worry.

b. There are different houses in cities and the country. Stilt houses are good in rainy places. They will stay dry in floods.

c. Stilt houses are not in the city or country. Apartment and farmhouses are not dry.

d. Cities and countries have houses. Too much rain causes floods but they stay high and dry.

Before you read

1. What would happen if the weather was always hot?

2. What would happen if it never rained?

VOCABULARY

flood n.
water that covers land not normally under water

rise v.
to move up

drought n.
a long time with little or no rain

desert n.
very dry area with few plants growing in it

desert

Extreme Weather

Around the world the weather is changing. Some places get too much rain and the ground cannot take in all the water. Other places are becoming too dry and there is not enough rain for plants to grow.

When there is too much rain, people worry about **floods**. In a flood, water **rises** up into streets and people's houses. People cannot move from place to place and some can die in the water.

If no rain falls for a long time, there can be **drought**. Then people worry about fires starting. Fires in dry places move quickly and can burn down forests and homes. Land with no rain can even turn to **desert** where very few plants and animals can live.

Scientists say this **extreme weather** is caused by **global warming**. Scientists say air all over the world is getting warmer. The temperature is rising. When warmer air moves over an area, it pulls moisture from the land. Wet earth then becomes dry. The warmer air takes the **moisture** to other places and the moisture falls to the earth as heavy rain.

Scientists worry about extreme weather because these problems are not going away. They are getting worse. Every year more places have fires, droughts, and floods. Scientists say **climate** around the world is changing.

extreme weather n.
weather that is not normal for a place, often causing harm

global warming n.
a rise in temperature around the Earth

moisture n.
wetness; water in the air

climate n.
the usual weather in a place

Vocabulary Builder

Fill in the Blank

▶ **Match each key word with its definition. Write the word in the blank.**

| desert | moisture | climate | global warming |

1. very dry area with few plants growing in it _______________

2. the usual weather in a place _______________

3. wetness; water in the air _______________

4. a rise in temperature around the Earth _______________

Complete the Sentence

▶ **Choose the word that best completes the sentence.**

1. The _______________ covered all the fields with water.
- **a.** chocolate
- **b.** flood
- **c.** happy
- **d.** warm

2. The airplane _______________ up into the air.
- **a.** sank
- **b.** rose
- **c.** ran
- **d.** fell

3. When the rain came the _______________ ended.
- **a.** flood
- **b.** moisture
- **c.** drought
- **d.** river

4. Floods and droughts are both kinds of _______________ .
- **a.** wet weather
- **b.** nice weather
- **c.** dry weather
- **d.** extreme weather

Main Idea & Details

▶ **Read the sentences below. Choose the best answer.**

1. The story is about _____________ . 
   a. hot weather   **b.** dry weather
   c. global warming   **d.** warming seas

2. People worry about _____________ in a drought. 
   a. floods coming   **b.** fires starting
   c. rain starting   **d.** fires going out

3. Scientists say the _____________ around the world is changing. 
   a. earth   **b.** water
   c. climate   **d.** moisture

Reading Comprehension

▶ **Circle T for true or F for false.**

1. Moisture falls as rain from warmer air.   T   F

2. Air around the world is getting cooler.   T   F

3. Extreme weather is a problem.   T   F

Summarizing

Summarize an article by only including the most important parts. A short summary can help you remember what happened more easily.

▶ **Read the sentences. Choose the ones with the most important information.**

1. **a.** The world's weather is changing with some places getting too much rain and others too little.

   b. The earth can't take all the water and then plants can't grow.

2. **a.** People can't move from place to place during floods.

   b. Too much rain causes floods where people could die.

3. **a.** When it doesn't rain, droughts deserts and forest fires can be a problem.

   b. Little can grow in the desert and forest fires spread fast.

4. **a.** Global warming is causing extreme weather as moisture moves with warm air.

   b. Warm air pulls moisture from the land when the temperature rises.

5. **a.** Scientists are worried by problems not going away.

   b. Extreme weather problems are getting worse as the world's climate changes.

READING SKILL

You can **paraphrase** a story by using different words.

What is written: A
Meaning: A

paraphrase →

What is written: B
Meaning: A

Skill Strategy The meaning should be the same even though you have changed the words used.

▶ **Read the article. Choose the sentences that best paraphrase what it says.**

Mount Vesuvius in Italy is a famous volcano. In 79 AD, hot mud came out of the volcano, killing many people.

When the mud cooled it looked like the people had been turned into stone. Even bread in the ovens that had been baking that day seemed to have turned to stone. We can still go to Pompeii to see these "statues" nearly two thousand years later.

1. Hot mud came out of Mount Vesuvius in 79 AD and ______________.

    a. made it a famous volcano

    b. killed most people in Pompeii

2. When the mud cooled ______________.

    a. bread cooking in ovens looked like it had turned to stone

    b. people stayed like stone statues for thousands of years

Before you read

1. Have you ever seen a volcano?
2. Would you like to live near one?

VOCABULARY

volcano n.
an opening in the earth's surface through which melted rock is forced out

erupt v.
to break or burst out suddenly

center n.
the middle

lava n.
hot liquid rock that erupts from a volcano

center

T 10

Volcanoes

Mountains may look like nothing more than huge pieces of rock. But some can be dangerous for people living near them. **Volcanoes** are usually cone-shaped mountains or hills that can cause a lot of damage if they **erupt**.

The **center** of the earth is full of hot liquid rock. Hot **lava** appears through weak spots in the earth's **surface** from deep beneath the ground. Lava flows out into the air where it cools and hardens to make new rocks. Volcanoes are made when this happens many times and the rock gets higher. Over time, the rock builds to make a small mountain and a volcano is formed.

Volcanic eruptions can kill many people. Lava can flow down the sides of a volcano onto the land below, **wrecking** homes and fields. So why do some people still choose to live near volcanoes? Cooled Lava left on the ground after an eruption can be very good for the soil. Lava is full of things that make the land **fertile** for farming.

Many old volcanoes will never erupt again. But there are still about 1,500 in the world that could. People living in volcanic areas such as Hawaii need to be ready to **evacuate** if a volcano is likely to erupt.

surface n.
the outside of something

wreck v.
to destroy something

fertile adj.
able to produce farm crops or other plants

evacuate v.
to leave a place for safety reasons

surface

Vocabulary Builder

Fill in the Blank

▶ **Match each key word with its definition. Write the word in the blank.**

center	erupt	surface	lava

1. to break or burst out suddenly   _______________

2. the outside of something   _______________

3. the middle   _______________

4. hot liquid rock that erupts from a volcano   _______________

Complete the Sentence

▶ **Choose the word that best completes the sentence.**

1. The train was _____________ after the accident.
    a. smiled   **b.** wrecked   **c.** fed   **d.** thanked

2. We had to _____________ the school building because there was a fire.
    a. evacuate   **b.** attend   **c.** drink   **d.** stay

3. The land was very _____________, so lots of flowers could grow.
    a. dry   **b.** flooded   **c.** fertile   **d.** dusty

4. The city was covered in lava when the _____________ erupted.
    a. bank   **b.** volcano   **c.** engine   **d.** people

Main Idea & Details

▶ **Read the sentences below. Choose the best answer.**

1. The article is about ____________ . 
- **a.** fertile land
- **b.** hot lava
- **c.** dangerous mountains
- **d.** volcanic eruptions

2. Volcanoes are usually ____________ mountains.
- **a.** very tall
- **b.** cone-shaped
- **c.** very small
- **d.** dome-shaped

3. There are still about 1,500 volcanoes in the world ____________ .
- **a.** that are not dangerous
- **b.** that will never erupt
- **c.** that are bigger than hills
- **d.** that could erupt

Reading Comprehension

▶ **Circle T for true or F for false.**

1. The center of the earth is cold hard rock.   T   F

2. Some people choose to live near volcanoes.   T   F

3. Hawaii is a volcanic area.   T   F

Paraphrasing

Tell the main points of an article in your own words to **paraphrase** it.
Keep just the important details, but don't put in your own ideas.

▶ **Read the sentences. Choose the sentence that best paraphrases each one.**

1. Lava flows out into the air where it cools and hardens to make new rocks. Volcanoes are made when this happens many times and the rock gets higher.
   a. Volcanoes form when cold lava builds up as rocks.
   b. Lava comes up many times into the air onto high rocks.
   c. Lava cooling in the air makes volcanoes many times.
   d. Cool hard rocks come from lava over and over again.

2. Cooled Lava left on the ground after an eruption can be very good for the soil. Lava is full of things that make the land fertile for farming.
   a. Lava will stay on farms and cool after eruptions.
   b. Eruptions are good for farming because of hot rock cools.
   c. Cool fertile ground is very good for the soil after lava erupts.
   d. Lava helps farmers because it makes soil fertile when it cools.

3. People living in volcanic areas such as Hawaii need to be ready to evacuate if a volcano is likely to erupt.
   a. Hawaii is one of the volcanic places where no one can ever live.
   b. Hawaiians must leave their homes if a volcano might erupt.
   c. People in Hawaii are always running from erupting volcanoes.
   d. There are other areas like Hawaii where volcanoes erupt.

READING SKILL

The things that happen in a story are called the **plot**.

Beginning → Middle → End

Skill Strategy The *beginning* tells about the characters and their problem. The *middle* is about how the characters try to solve the problem. The *end* tells you how everything works out.

▶ **Read the story. Think about the main points that make the plot.**

Narcissus was very handsome. Many girls fell in love with him, but Narcissus laughed and made them cry.

One day Narcissus saw his face in the water of a pond and he fell in love with it! When he tried to touch the face in the water it just disappeared.

He looked and looked but he could never touch the face. He did not eat or sleep. He became thin and lost his good looks!

Beginning	**1.** Narcissus _______________ . **a.** was very handsome **b.** made girls cry
Middle	**2.** Narcissus _______________ his face in the water of a pond. **a.** fell in love with **b.** tried to touch
End	**3.** Narcissus _______________ . **a.** looked and looked **b.** lost his good looks

LESSON 11

PLOT
Language Arts

Before you read

1. Did you ever wish you could fly?
2. Do you think flying would be scary?

VOCABULARY

prisoner n.
a person who has been caught or locked up

evil adj.
having a very bad character or behavior

escape v.
to get away from a place you are being kept

clever adj.
having a quick mind, smart

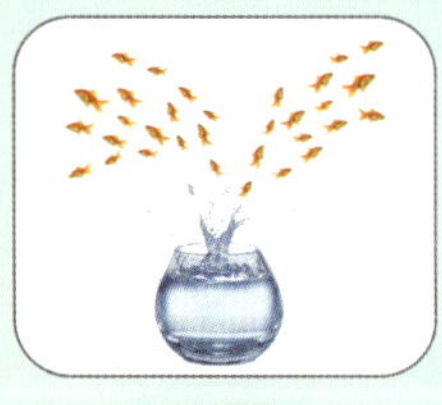

escape

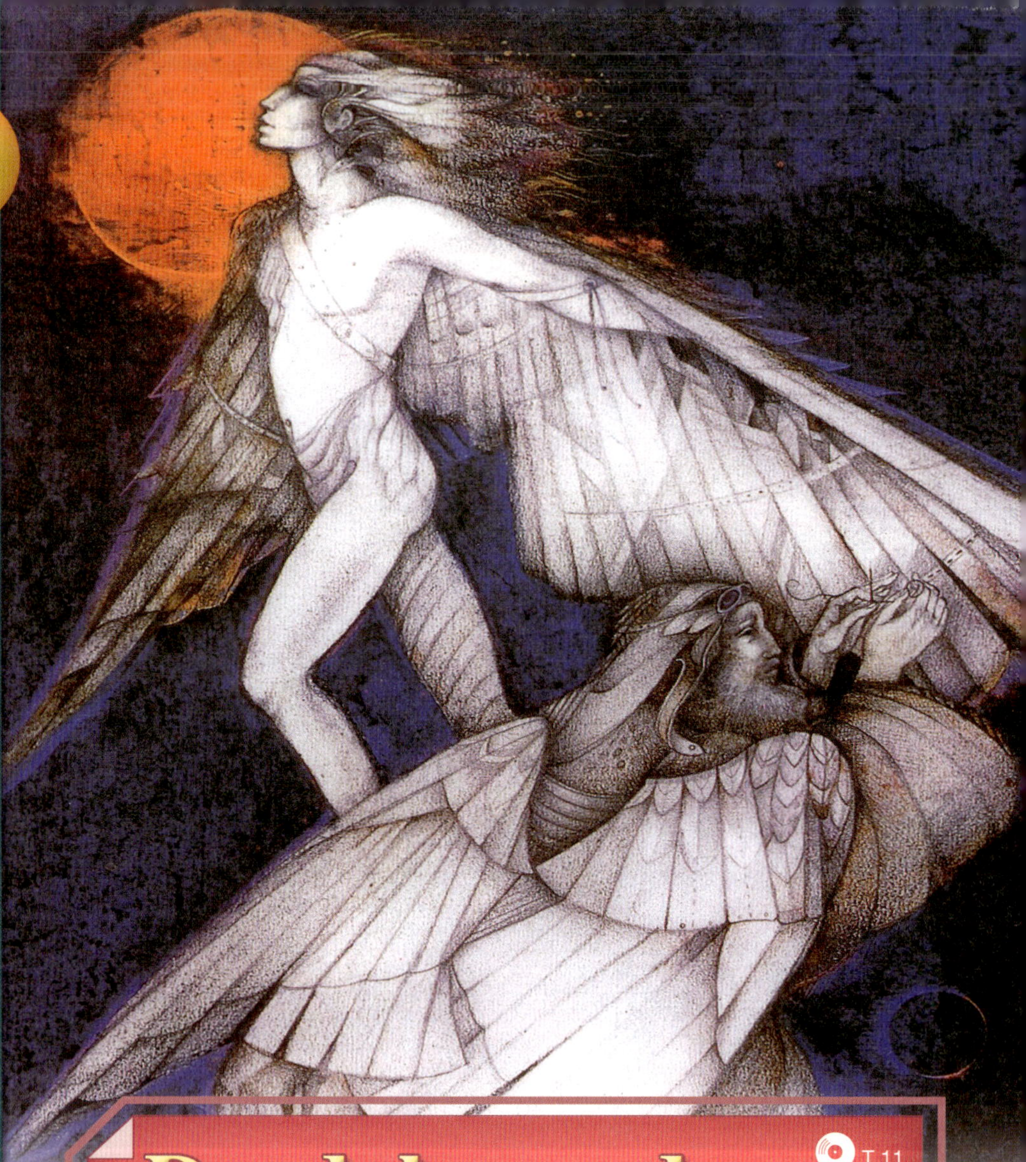

Daedalus and Icarus

T 11

Daedalus and his son Icarus were **prisoners**. The **evil** King Minos kept them in a tall tower on the Greek island of Crete. They wanted to **escape** and return to their home in the city of Athens.

Daedalus was a very **clever** man, and thought hard about how they could get away. He saw the birds flying outside. He stuck feathers to sticks using wax to make wings. They could fly away from the tower. Daedalus and Icarus tied the giant wings to their backs.

Daedalus **warned** Icarus: "Do not fly too **close** to the sea. If you do you might fall in. Do not fly too close to the sun, either. If you do the hot sun will melt the wax on your wings." Daedalus and Icarus jumped and flew away. Soon, Icarus got bored and wanted to fly higher, close to the sun.

He flew up into the air, but the sun was so hot that the wax on his wings began to melt. The feathers started falling off one by one. Soon there were not enough feathers left. He **flapped** and flapped, but he could not stay in the air. He fell into the **ocean**. He should have listened to Daedalus' warning not to fly too close to the sun!

warn v.
to tell about possible harm or danger

close adj.
near in space or time

flap v.
to move arms or wings quickly up and down

ocean n.
part of the body of salt water that covers the earth

warn

Vocabulary Builder

Fill in the Blank

▶ **Match each key word with its definition. Write the word in the blank.**

ocean	evil	prisoner	escape

1. to get away from a place you are being kept _______________

2. a person who has been caught or locked up _______________

3. having a very bad character or behavior _______________

4. part of the body of salt water that covers the earth _______________

Complete the Sentence

▶ **Choose the word that best completes the sentence.**

1. The fireman _______________ people to be careful with matches.
   a. chatted **b.** stamped **c.** warned **d.** signed

2. The bird _______________ its wings to fly.
   a. rested **b.** flapped **c.** folded **d.** borrowed

3. My house is very _______________ to the school.
   a. far **b.** right **c.** close **d.** left

4. My brother is so _______________ . He always gets good grades.
   a. silly **b.** clever **c.** lazy **d.** sleepy

Main Idea & Details

▶ **Read the sentences below. Choose the best answer.**

1. The story is about ______________.
   a. Daedalus making wings to escape
   b. Icarus flying too close to the sun
   c. an evil king keeping people prisoner
   d. Daedalus giving Icarus a warning

2. Daedalus warns Icarus ______________.
   a. not to fly near the sun   **b.** to fly very close to the sea
   c. not to flap too hard   **d.** to always fly very high in the sky

3. The sun could ______________.
   a. make Icarus hot and tired   **b.** melt the wax on the wings
   c. heat the water in the ocean   **d.** show them the way to Athens

Reading Comprehension

▶ **Circle T for true or F for false.**

1. Daedalus and Icarus liked living in the tall tower.   T   F

2. The sun made the wax on Icarus' wings melt.   T   F

3. Icarus' home city was Athens.   T   F

Plot

The beginning, middle, and end of a story make the **plot**. The beginning introduces characters and problems, the middle tells how they try to solve them, and the end tells if the story has a happy or sad conclusion.

▶ **Read the phrases in the box. Write the correct letters in the blanks to tell the main points of the plot's beginning, middle and end.**

> **a.** sad
> **b.** making wings to escape
> **c.** Daedalus and Icarus
> **d.** prisoners in a tower
> **e.** falls in the ocean
> **f.** flies too close to the sun

Beginning	**1.** The main characters are ____________ . **2.** The problem is that they are ____________ .
Middle	**3.** Daedalus tries to solve their problem by **4.** But Icarus ____________ .
End	**5.** There is a ____________ ending. **6.** Icarus ____________ .

LESSON 12 Fact and Opinion

READING SKILL

A **fact** is something that is true. An **opinion** is one person's thoughts or feelings.

Fact	Opinion
(can be proved to be true or false)	(cannot be proved to be true or false)

Signal Words *I like, I agree, I disagree, I think, I believe, In my opinion* are clues for opinion.

▶ **Read the article. Then choose fact or opinion.**

People all over the world eat pizza. They put cheese, meat, tomatoes, and vegetables on pizza dough. Then they bake it all in an oven. Antonio thinks pepperoni pizza tastes good. He eats it every week. He likes pepperoni pizza most. He believes it tastes best with lots of cheese.

1. People all over the world eat pizza.   **Fact**   **Opinion**

2. Pepperoni pizza tastes good.   **Fact**   **Opinion**

3. Antonio eats pizza every week.   **Fact**   **Opinion**

FACT AND OPINION
Social Studies

Before you read

1. Do you like pizza?
2. What kind of pizza do you like best?

VOCABULARY

business n.
the work a person does to earn money

hometown n.
the place where a person was born or grew up

coast n.
the land next to the ocean or large lakes

proud adj.
feeling good about oneself because of something

Pizza-Maker

T 12

Everyone in my family makes and sells pizza. My grandparents made pizza and their parents also made pizza. Pizza is our family **business**.

We come from northern Italy. Our **hometown** is Malcesine. I lived there for 11 years. I think Malcesine is a beautiful town. It is on the east **coast** of Lake Garda, the largest lake in Italy. I am **proud** to come from there because **historians** think it is where the first pizza was made.

The first pizza was made thousands of years ago, when people started adding **ingredients** to bread. They thought putting tomatoes on top of the bread tasted good.

I don't live near Lake Garda any more, though. After my eleventh birthday, my family moved to New York. **Nowadays**, I help make and sell pizzas in our pizzeria in New York City.

Pizzas came to New York when the first Italian people moved there about 200 years ago. People in America thought that pizza was delicious, but they changed the **recipe** over time. Nowadays, New York pizza has a thick base, but Italian pizza is thin. Both kinds of pizza are famous and delicious in their own way.

Fill in the Blank

▶ **Match each key word with its definition. Write the word in the blank.**

| nowadays   hometown   business   historian |

1. a person who studies history　　　　　　　__________________

2. the work a person does to earn money　　__________________

3. at this present time　　　　　　　　　　__________________

4. the place where a person was born or grew up　__________________

Complete the Sentence

▶ **Choose the word that best completes the sentence.**

1. She used a _____________ to bake the cake.

   a. recipe　　　　**b.** fan　　　　**c.** plant　　　　**d.** shoe

2. The main _____________ in cheese is milk.

   a. recipe　　　　**b.** ingredient　　　**c.** art　　　　**d.** spoon

3. We went on holiday to the _____________ because we wanted to see the sea.

   a. desert　　　　**b.** mountain　　　**c.** coast　　　　**d.** park

4. I was _____________ when I got an A in English.

   a. angry　　　　**b.** silly　　　　**c.** proud　　　　**d.** sad

Comprehension Check

Main Idea & Details

▶ **Read the sentences below. Choose the best answer.**

1. This story is about someone who ______________ .
- **a.** lives in Malcesine
- **b.** eats pizzas
- **c.** is a historian
- **d.** makes pizzas

2. The first pizza was made in ______________ .
- **a.** New York two hundred years ago
- **b.** Europe two hundred years ago
- **c.** Europe thousands of years ago
- **d.** New York thousands of years ago

3. New York pizza has a ________ than Italian pizza.
- **a.** saltier taste
- **b.** thicker base
- **c.** thinner base
- **d.** sweeter taste

Reading Comprehension

▶ **Circle T for true or F for false.**

1. We moved to New York when I was twelve.　　T　F

2. I help make and sell pizzas in New York.　　T　F

3. New York pizzas have more cheese on them than Italian pizza.　T　F

Fact and Opinion

Some sentences tell **facts**. A fact can be proved true. Other sentences tell people's **opinions**. An opinion tells how a person thinks or feels.

▶ **Read each sentence. Then tick the correct box.**

		FACT	OPINION
1.	Pizza is our family business.		
2.	Malcesine is on the coast of Lake Garda.		
3.	Malcesine is a beautiful town.		
4.	Moved from Italy to New York.		
5.	I make and sell pizzas in a pizzeria.		
6.	Both New York and Italian pizzas are delicious.		

▶ **Read the sentences. Write the opinion words in the box.**

1. My grandparents made delicious pizzas. ____________

2. I am a proud pizza-maker from Lake Garda. ____________

Comparing and Contrasting

READING SKILL

Comparing shows how things are alike.
Contrasting shows how things are different.

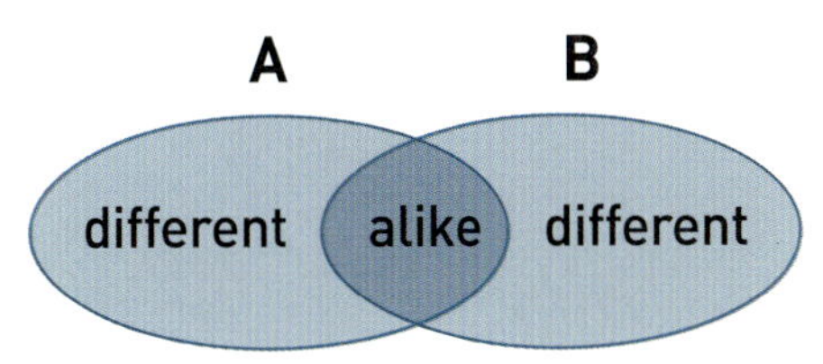

Signal Words *Same*, *both* and *like* help you to compare things. *Different*, *however* and *but* can help show contrasts.

▶ **Read the article. Then choose the correct word to complete each sentence and say if it is a compare or contrast word.**

Frank used to send real Christmas cards to his family and friends each year. He wrote them by hand and took them to the post office. However, after Christmas people threw the cards away, making lots of waste. This year, Frank sent e-cards by email. The e-cards had the same messages and pictures as real cards but didn't use paper. Also, Frank didn't need to go to the post office!

1. The real cards and e-cards had (the same / different) Christmas messages.

   a. compare   **b.** contrast

2. Real cards use paper (but / like) e-cards don't.

   a. compare   **b.** contrast

3. Frank had to go to the post office with real cards, but E-cards were (like / different).

   a. compare   **b.** contrast

COMPARING AND CONTRASTING
Social Studies

Before you read

1. Do you speak to your friends every day?
2. How do you contact them?

VOCABULARY

contact v.
to speak or write to someone

send v.
to cause to go

cell phone n.
a mobile telephone that works with no wires

message n.
a piece of information sent or given to someone

contact

T 13

Communications

Nowadays, people can **contact** each other quickly in many ways. They can **send** an email, call using a **cell phone** or send a text. We can speak to our friends and family very easily. In the past it took a lot longer to send a **message** to other people!

In America people used to send letters if they wanted to contact each other.

Wagons first went on the San Antonio - San Diego Mail Line in 1857. Wagons went 1,500 miles between

San Antonio, Texas and San Diego, California every two months. It took them 30 days, so people waited a month to get a letter!

Then, Samuel Morse invented the **long-distance** telegraph. Telegraphs were used all over America by 1861. The first line went 40 miles from Washington to Baltimore. It sent electric messages

down a **wire** quickly over long distances. People could send up to 50 words a minute. But the messages were much shorter than letters taken by wagon.

Next, the telephone helped people to contact each other over long distances. Alexander Graham Bell invented it in 1876. The telephone was quick, like telegraphs, but people could speak to each other **instead of** sending written messages.

We still use telephones today, even though we have email and cell phones too. However, we don't use wagons and telegraphs anymore!

Vocabulary Builder

Fill in the Blank

▶ **Match each key word with its definition. Write the word in the blank.**

wagon	contact	wire	instead of

1. a vehicle with four wheels often pulled by horses ________________

2. in place of something else ________________

3. a long, thin thread of metal ________________

4. to speak or write to someone ________________

Complete the Sentence

▶ **Choose the word that best completes the sentence.**

1. I wrote you a ____________ and left it on your desk.

   a. phone call   **b.** message   **c.** cell phone   **d.** telegram

2. If I ____________ my brother a letter he will write back to me.

   a. tell   **b.** call   **c.** send   **d.** keep

3. She could hear her ____________ ringing in her bag.

   a. watch   **b.** wallet   **c.** makeup   **d.** cell phone

4. The ____________ flight went from Los Angeles to London.

   a. short-distance   **b.** long-distance   **c.** local   **d.** Asian

Comprehension Check

Main Idea & Details

▶ **Read the sentences below. Choose the best answer.**

1. The article is about a(n) ____________ . 
   - **a.** sending letters by wagon to friends
   - **b.** different ways of contacting people
   - **c.** sending telegraphs to your family
   - **d.** sending text messages with your cell phone

2. It took ____________ to send a letter on the San Antonio - San Diego Mail Line.
   - **a.** one week
   - **b.** one month
   - **c.** one year
   - **d.** one day

3. The first long-distance telegraph went from ____________ .
   - **a.** Washington to Baltimore
   - **b.** California to Texas
   - **c.** San Diego to Baltimore
   - **d.** San Antonio to Washington

Reading Comprehension

▶ **Circle T for true or F for false.**

1. Alexander Graham Bell invented the telegraph.   T   F

2. Telegraph messages were longer than letters.   T   F

3. We don't use wagons and telegrams now.   T   F

Comparing and Contrasting

Think about how things you read about are alike and different.
Compare them with words such as **same**, **all** and **like**. **Contrast** with words such as **different**, **however** and **but**.

▶ **Write the correct letters to complete the sentences. Then tick the correct box.**

a. like
b. different
c. but
d. all

	comparing	contrasting
1. Mail wagons, telegraphs and telephones ____________ helped people contact each other over long distances.		
2. It could take 30 days to send a message on a wagon, ____________ a telegraph could be sent in minutes.		
3. ____________ a telegraph, a telephone call was a quick way to contact people.		
4. Using a telephone was ____________ from telegraphs because people could speak to each other instead of sending written messages.		

LESSON 14 Point of View

READING SKILL

The same story can sound different when told from different **points of view**.

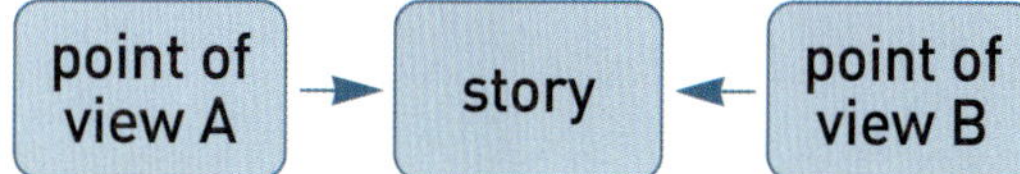

Skill Strategy People in the story can use words like *I* and *my*. An outside narrator can use *he*, *she*, *it* or *they*.

▶ **Read the article. Then choose the correct speaker.**

Sam and Betty are very close friends, but they also need each other for different things!

Sam: "Most dogs are not allowed to go inside the supermarket, but I am because I am a guide dog! I am there to help my owner, Betty, because she cannot see."

Betty: "I could not go to the supermarket alone before I got my guide dog. I feed Sam every day and he acts as my eyes when I go out. He helps me find my way even though I cannot see."

1. "Sam and Betty are very close friends, but they also need each other for different things!"

    a. Sam   **b.** Betty   **c.** an outside narrator

2. "I am there to help my owner, Betty, because she cannot see."

    a. Sam   **b.** Betty   **c.** an outside narrator

Before you read

1. Do you like dogs?
2. Would you like to work with one as your partner?

VOCABULARY

handler n.
a person who trains and works with animals

partner n.
the one who someone works or does business with

badge n.
a pin worn to show someone's job, or the group they belong to

vest n.
a special piece of clothing worn on the upper body

vest

Sniffing Out Crime

T 14

Being in the police force can be a difficult job, but people are not the only ones who can help keep their city safe. Dogs, called K-9s, are used to help police officers. The New York Police Department (NYPD) has 30 German Shepherds in its K-9 unit. They help human police officers to fight crime.

Brian: "My name is Brian and I am a NYPD dog **handler**. My **partner** is a German Shepherd called Rufus. He has his own police **badge** and even wears a special police **vest** to stop anything harming him when he is working. He has caught a lot of people wanted by the police.

He is seven years old, so next year he will give up work and I will get a new dog."

Rufus: "My name is Rufus and I love working for the NYPD. I have a stronger sense of smell than humans so I can **sniff out** crime on the streets of New York. I have **chased** people running away from the police and even helped find **missing** people and things. Seven is quite old for a dog, though, so I will **retire** next year. Then, I will live with a family and chase rabbits instead of people."

chase

Vocabulary Builder

Fill in the Blank

▶ **Match each key word with its definition. Write the word in the blank.**

retire	missing	sniff out	handler

1. unable to be found   _______________

2. to stop a job because of age   _______________

3. to find something by smelling   _______________

4. a person who trains and works with animal   _______________

Complete the Sentence

▶ **Choose the word that best completes the sentence.**

1. My dog likes to _____________ cats but he never catches them.
   - **a.** brush
   - **b.** chase
   - **c.** lick
   - **d.** stroke

2. I wear a _____________ to show that I am a Boy Scout.
   - **a.** letter
   - **b.** book
   - **c.** promise
   - **d.** badge

3. Wearing a life _____________ can save you if you fall into the sea.
   - **a.** shirt
   - **b.** hat
   - **c.** vest
   - **d.** visor

4. Let me call my business _____________ to finish the deal.
   - **a.** partner
   - **b.** wife
   - **c.** pupil
   - **d.** school

Main Idea & Details

▶ **Read the sentences below. Choose the best answer.**

1. The article is about a(n) ______________ . 
   a. dogs in the police force   **b.** retired police dogs
   c. police dog handlers   **d.** ways to sniff out crime

2. Rufus wears a special vest to ______________ .
   a. show that he is a police dog
   b. help him smell out missing people
   c. stop him getting hurt when working
   d. help him chase wanted people

3. Rufus has ______________ .
   a. no partner in the NYPD   **b.** caught a lot of people
   c. not enjoyed his job   **d.** a long time left as a police dog

Reading Comprehension

▶ **Circle T for true or F for false.**

1. Rufus will retire next year.   T   F

2. Brian has a better sense of smell than Rufus.   T   F

3. Right now, Rufus mostly chases rabbits.   T   F

Point of View

Characters can use words like **I** and **my** to give their first-person point of view. An outside narrator can also speak from the third-person point of view using words like **he**, **she**, **it** or **they**.

▶ **Read the sentences. Choose the correct answers.**

> They help human police officers to fight crime.

1. This is told by ____________ .

   a. Rufus   **b.** Brian   **c.** an outside narrator

2. It is told from the (first-person / third-person) point of view.

> My partner is a German Shepherd called Rufus.

3. This is told by ____________ .

   a. Rufus   **b.** Brian   **c.** an outside narrator

4. It is told from the (first-person / third-person) point of view.

> I have a stronger sense of smell than humans so I can help Brian sniff out crime on the streets New York.

5. This is told by ____________ .

   a. Rufus   **b.** Brian   **c.** an outside narrator

6. It is told from the (first-person / third-person) point of view.

LESSON 15 Character

▶ **Read the article. Match the sentences.**

The artist Vincent van Gogh was born in 1853. One of his most famous pictures was called Sunflowers. It showed bright yellow flowers. Van Gogh painted wonderful pictures, but he was not always a happy character. Even as a child, van Gogh was quiet and thought a lot. When he was older, his neighbors heard him crying at night. However, people still remember van Gogh as a great artist.

What we know van Gogh did	What it says about van Gogh
1. He painted wonderful pictures.	**a.** He was serious.
2. He was quiet and thought a lot.	**b.** He was sad.
3. He was heard crying at night.	**c.** He was a great artist.

CHARACTER
Art

Before you read

1. Do you like paintings?

2. Do you like paintings of people or places best?

VOCABULARY

talented adj.
being very good at something

artist n.
a person skilled in painting, music, or other arts

statue n.
a piece of art usually made from stone or metal

invent v.
to make something never made before

artist

Mona Lisa

🔊 T 15

Leonardo da Vinci was a very **talented** man and a great **artist** who lived in the 16th century. People who knew him said he had many friends and was interested in everything. He painted pictures, made **statues**, wrote books and **invented** machines.

Da Vinci's painting the Mona Lisa is still loved today. He painted it in Florence, a city in Italy. For centuries, people did not know who the **portrait** was of. But most art-lovers now think it is

a picture of a woman called Lisa del Giocondo.

Lisa was a married woman with six children who lived in Florence. Her husband asked the artist to paint her portrait. The portrait was called "the happy one" as well as the Mona Lisa because of Lisa's **mysterious** smile.

The picture became very famous because everyone **wondered** about Lisa's smile. What was she thinking? What did it say about her character?

Art **historians** say the painting shows that Lisa was a good wife. In the 16th century, women were painted with their hands held together to show they were faithful to their husbands. She also has expensive clothes on to make her look rich. The painting is very big and expensive — also showing that Lisa and her husband wanted people to think they were rich.

Vocabulary Builder

Fill in the Blank

▶ **Match each key word with its definition. Write the word in the blank.**

mysterious	historian	portrait	invent

1. not known or explained   _______________

2. to make something never made before   _______________

3. a person whose job is to study history   _______________

4. a painting, drawing, photograph or statue of a person   _______________

Complete the Sentence

▶ **Choose the word that best completes the sentence.**

1. There was a stone _____________ of the king in the museum.
   a. painting   **b.** photograph   **c.** song   **d.** statue

2. He was a _____________ cook so dinner always tasted great.
   a. poor   **b.** talented   **c.** bad   **d.** lazy

3. The _____________ painted a beautiful picture.
   a. baby   **b.** statue   **c.** artist   **d.** runner

4. I _____________ what I will get for my birthday.
   a. clue   **b.** wonder   **c.** mystery   **d.** artist

Main Idea & Details

▶ **Read the sentences below. Choose the best answer.**

1. The article is about a(n) ______________ . *Main Idea*
   a. Leonardo da Vinci
   c. the Mona Lisa
   b. the 16th century
   d. Florence in Italy

2. The painting the Mona Lisa is famous for ______________ . *Details*
   a. the mysterious smile
   c. being so old
   b. being so big
   d. costing a lot

3. The real Lisa was ______________ . *Details*
   a. a silk seller
   c. not married
   b. married with six children
   d. an artist

Reading Comprehension

▶ **Circle T for true or F for false.**

1. Leonardo da Vinci had few friends.   T   F

2. Leonardo da Vinci was only good at painting.   T   F

3. The Mona Lisa was also called "the happy one."   T   F

Focus on Skill

Character

Think about what is written about a person in a story or article. Think about what they say and do. Think about what the author and other people say about them.

▶ **Read the sentences from the story. Choose the correct word to show what each says about the character in it.**

1. He painted pictures, made statues, wrote books and invented machines.
This sentence shows da Vinci was very ____________ .

   a. friendly   **b.** happy   **c.** rich   **d.** talented

2. Everyone wondered about Lisa's smile.
This sentence shows Lisa del Giocondo was a ____________ .

   a. good wife   **b.** mysterious woman
   c. rich wife   **d.** great artist

▶ **Choose the correct answer to complete each sentence about different characters.**

1. We can tell da Vinci was a great artist because ____________ .

   a. his painting the Mona Lisa is still loved today.
   b. he had a lot of friends
   c. he made statues and wrote books
   d. he painted in Florence, a city in Italy.

2. We can tell Lisa was a good wife because she ____________ .

   a. was called "the happy one"   **b.** had a mysterious smile
   c. held her hands together   **d.** was wearing expensive clothes

LESSON 16 Author's Purpose

READING SKILL

The reason for writing is the **author's purpose**. The author can have more than one purpose.

Skill Strategy Authors may write *to teach* or *entertain*. They may want the readers to *believe something* or *act in a certain way*.

▶ **Read about a special day in the United States. Think about why the author wrote about it.**

November 15th is America Recycles Day. People across the United States teach each other about recycling. Recycling is taking used things, like old newspapers, and changing them into new things, like new paper. On November 15th, people find out what can be recycled. They also learn when, where, and how to recycle. America Recycles Day helps Americans make their country more beautiful.

Choose the correct answer.

The author wants to ______________ .

    a. tell about Americans and their country

    b. make you want to learn about recycling

    c. teach about America Recycles Day

Before you read

1. Do you recycle every day?
2. Could you do more to make less trash?

VOCABULARY

environment n.
the natural world

trash n.
anything thrown away because it is not wanted

reduce v.
to make less in amount or size

throw away phrase
to put something not wanted in a place that takes it away

The 3Rs

My name is Jane and I am an American middle school student. I have a special job at my school. I teach other students how to care for the **environment**. Too much **trash** harms the environment, so I teach kids at my school about the 3Rs.

The first R means **reduce**. Reduce by making less trash. Don't buy things you can use only once and then **throw away**. For example, don't buy paper plates use real ones. Don't buy things that have been **packaged** too much. For example, buy cookies that come in one big box. Don't always buy many small boxes of cookies.

The second R means **reuse**. Reuse by using things more than one time. For example, use paper and plastic bags over and over again. Another way to reuse is by giving **stuff** away. For example, give your old clothes, books, and toys to someone else to use.

The third R means **recycle**. Recycle by putting things that can be recycled into special containers. Recycle newspapers, magazines, and cardboard boxes. Cans, plastic bottles, and glass bottles can also be recycled. When old things get recycled, new things can be made from the old ones.

Now you know about the 3Rs. It's your turn to help save the environment!

package v.
to put in a box or wrap in plastic

reuse v.
to use again or more than once

stuff n.
things or objects

recycle v.
to take used things and change them into new things

package

Fill in the Blank

▶ **Match each key word with its definition. Write the word in the blank.**

environment	reduce	reuse	package

1. the natural world ________________

2. to put in a box or wrap in plastic ________________

3. to make less in amount or size ________________

4. to use again or more than once ________________

Complete the Sentence

▶ **Choose the word that best completes the sentence.**

1. We have to pick up ____________ in our schoolyard.
   a. sun　　　　**b.** rain　　　　**c.** trash　　　　**d.** music

2. Don't ____________ the pasta. I want to eat more!
   a. make more of　**b.** throw away　**c.** give me　　**d.** show me

3. We should ____________ glass and plastic so that we can use it again.
   a. recycle　　　**b.** read　　　　**c.** plant　　　　**d.** tell

4. This box is too heavy. It has too much ____________ in it.
   a. air　　　　　**b.** sun　　　　　**c.** stuff　　　　**d.** nothing

✔ Comprehension Check

Main Idea & Details

▶ **Read the sentences below. Choose the best answer.**

1. The article is about a(n) ____________ .
   a. the environment
   b. the 3Rs
   c. trash
   d. a student

2. Students can reduce trash by ____________ .
   a. buying packaged things
   b. throwing away lots of things
   c. not buying paper plates
   d. not eating cookies

3. Students can reuse things by ____________ .
   a. using stuff only one time
   b. giving stuff to someone else
   c. keeping all of their stuff
   d. putting old stuff in paper and plastic bags

Reading Comprehension

▶ **Circle T for true or F for false.**

1. Jane teaches other students the 3Rs: how to read, write, and review. **T F**

2. One way to reuse things is by using plastic bags again and again. **T F**

3. Newspapers, magazines, and cardboard boxes can be recycled. **T F**

Author's Purpose

When you read, think about why the author is writing. Sometimes they want to tell you something. They may also want to teach you something. Sometimes it is just for fun.

▶ **Choose the correct answer.**

The author wrote the article to ______________.

a. tell you a funny story about Jane and make you laugh
b. teach ways to help the environment
c. make you buy recycled things
d. make you want to eat boxes of cookies

▶ **Write the correct letters in the blanks to give the reason they were written.**

What the author says	The author's purpose
______ **1.** My name is Jane and I am a middle school student.	**a.** To explain R number 2.
______ **2.** Too much trash harms the environment.	**b.** To say who she is.
______ **3.** The 3Rs: Reduce, Reuse, Recycle	**c.** To explain R number 1.
______ **4.** The first R means reduce.	**d.** To ask you to do the 3Rs too.
______ **5.** The second R means reuse.	**e.** To say why too much trash is bad.
______ **6.** The third R means recycle.	**f.** To name the three Rs.
______ **7.** Please follow them and help save the environment!	**g.** To explain R number 3.

LESSON 17 Setting

READING SKILL

The **setting** is where(place) and when(time) a story happens.

Skill Strategy Characters act differently as the setting changes.

▶ **Read the article. Choose the correct answer.**

People normally go snowboarding on snowy mountains. They wear a lot of clothes to keep out the cold and wet snow.

But you can also go sandboarding in the desert! People stand on a board and are pulled along by a car over sand. But they have to be in the hot, dry air and sand to do it.

The two sports might use similar skills but the setting is very different.

1. The setting for snowboarding is in the ______________ snowy mountains.

    a. cold and dry   **b.** cold and wet

    c. hot and dry   **d.** hot and wet

2. The setting for sandboarding is in the ______________ sandy desert.

    a. cold and dry   **b.** cold and wet

    c. hot and dry   **d.** hot and wet

Before you read

1. What date is Christmas Day?

2. Is it usually cold or hot in your country on Christmas Day?

VOCABULARY

opposite adj.
at the other end, side, or corner of something

normal adj.
usual or ordinary; not strange

almost adv.
only a little less than; nearly

snowmobile n.
a vehicle used for traveling on snow or ice

snowmobile

T 17

Two Christmases

Isabella and David were friends, but they lived at **opposite** ends of the world. So they sent each other an email once a week. Last week was Christmas day so they had a lot to tell each other about their celebrations.

First Isabella wrote: "Winter is even colder than **normal** in Alaska this year. We had **almost** eight meters of snow on the ground, so my uncle came to our house for Christmas on his **snowmobile**! We opened presents around the fire, so we would feel warm even though it was freezing outside.

I got some great skis for my Christmas, but the best gift would be some warm sunshine again. In winter, the sun only shines for five hours a day in Alaska! It is mostly dark. However, in the summer we will have almost twenty hours of sunlight!"

Then it was David's turn to **reply**. He wrote: "Wow your Christmas was very different from mine! It is the middle of summer in Australia so it's very sunny. Actually, it is too hot for me! We need to turn on our **air conditioner** to keep cool! I met my **relatives** on the beautiful sandy beach and my aunt gave me a new **surfboard**. We had a fire, too, but of course it wasn't to keep warm. It was a BBQ."

Vocabulary Builder

Fill in the Blank

▶ **Match each key word with its definition. Write the word in the blank.**

| surfboard | snowmobile | opposite | air conditioner |

1. at the other end, side, or corner of something ______________

2. a vehicle used for traveling on snow or ice ______________

3. a long, narrow board used to ride on ocean waves ______________

4. a machine to keep air in a room at a comfortable temperature ______________

Complete the Sentence

▶ **Choose the word that best completes the sentence.**

1. My mother sent me a letter last week but I didn't __________ yet.

a. sign　　**b.** call　　**c.** reply　　**d.** tell

2. It's __________ time for the TV show to start. We can watch it in ten minutes.

a. never　　**b.** almost　　**c.** past　　**d.** later

3. Once a year, all my __________ visit my grandmother for a family party.

a. relatives　　**b.** friends　　**c.** classmates　　**d.** teachers

4. It is __________ to have snow in winter in Alaska.

a. strange　　**b.** unusual　　**c.** odd　　**d.** normal

Comprehension Check

Main Idea & Details

▶ **Read the sentences below. Choose the best answer.**

1. The story is about two ____________ . 
- **a.** friends writing emails
- **b.** different Christmas gifts
- **c.** kinds of weather
- **d.** different Christmases

2. The days in Alaska are ____________ .
- **a.** long in winter
- **b.** short in winter
- **c.** short in summer
- **d.** the same all year round

3. The weather at Christmas in Australia is ____________ .
- **a.** very hot and dry
- **b.** very cold and snowy
- **c.** cool and fresh
- **d.** a little rainy and warm

Reading Comprehension

▶ **Circle T for true or F for false.**

1. Isabella likes having short days in winter.   T   F

2. Christmas time is in the Australian summer.   T   F

3. Both Isabella and David had fires on Christmas day.   T   F

Setting

Setting tells where and when a story happens. The story can happen anywhere at any time. Think about the setting to understand the characters' lives.

▶ **Choose the correct answers to complete each sentence.**

1. It is (summer / winter) in Alaska and (summer / winter) in Australia.

2. Isabella's fire in Alaska was used to (cook food / keep people warm).

3. David's fire in Australia was used to (cook food / keep people warm).

▶ **Tick Australia or Alaska to say which setting words from the passage describe.**

	Alaska	Australia
1. sandy		
2. mostly dark		
3. very sunny		
4. too hot		
5. freezing outside		
6. snowy		

READING SKILL

A **map** is a picture of a particular area that shows you where things are.

Skill Strategy A map can have a *map key*, *label*, and *compass rose*.

▶ **Look at the map. Then choose the correct answers.**

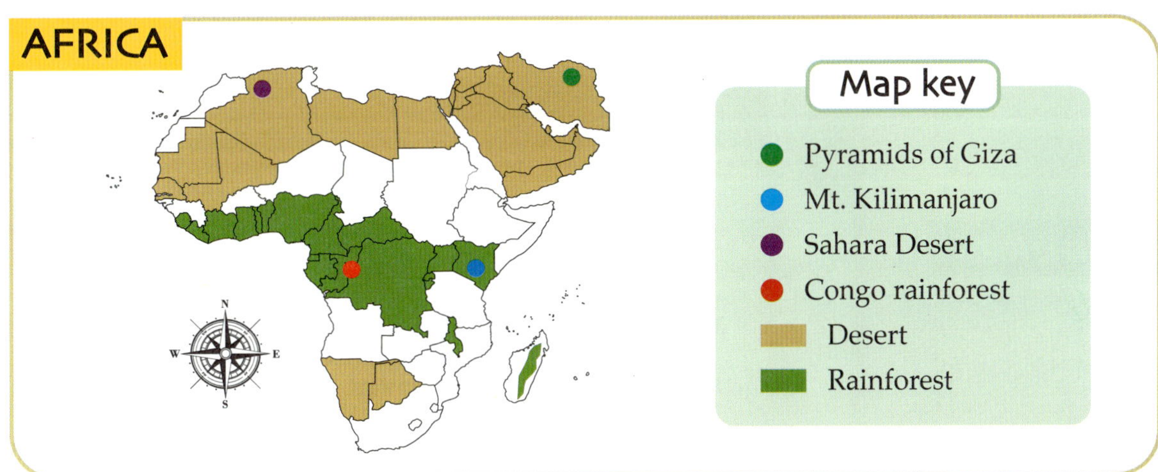

1. Which two places are in the north of Africa?

   a. Pyramids of Giza   **b.** Mt. Kilimanjaro

   c. Sahara Desert   **d.** Congo rainforest

2. A large part of Africa's rainforest is to the _____________ of the Sahara Desert.

   a. north   **b.** east   **c.** south   **d.** west

Before you read

1. What foreign countries have you visited?

2. What foreign countries you want to visit?

Trip to Asia

I am only twelve years old, but I have the best job in the world! I **travel** the world. I don't go **alone**, though. My parents take me. They are photographers. People pay them to take pictures of things in different countries. If they go on a **trip** somewhere, I go, too.

This summer was **fantastic**! We traveled around Asia taking pictures. Did you know that Asia is the largest area of land in the world? It's huge, with many different kinds of countries.

The first place we **visited** was in Iraq. We went to the Great Mosque of Samarra. I had fun climbing up the giant tower.

Next we traveled southeast to India. We went to the Taj Mahal. A king built the Taj Mahal for his wife after she died. He must have loved her a lot!

Then we flew northeast to China in an airplane. We went to the Great Wall of China. I wanted to walk the **whole** thing, but I couldn't. It is more than 6,000 kilometers long.

We went to Cambodia for the last part of our journey. My parents wanted to take pictures of the Angkor temples. There are over 100 temples!

I learn a lot about **geography**, and I always have fun. Traveling is a great **adventure**!

Vocabulary Builder

Fill in the Blank

▶ **Match each key word with its definition. Write the word in the blank.**

| fantastic | alone | whole | adventure |

1. excellent, wonderful   _______________

2. having the entire amount or length   _______________

3. without anyone or anything else   _______________

4. a trip or activity that is dangerous or exciting   _______________

Complete the Sentence

▶ **Choose the word that best completes the sentence.**

1. My father is going on a business ____________ next week.

   a. alone   **b.** geography   **c.** trip   **d.** whole

2. My grandparents always ____________ us for the holidays.

   a. visit   **b.** geography   **c.** trip   **d.** travel

3. We study ____________ to learn about places around the world.

   a. math   **b.** science   **c.** English   **d.** geography

4. I can't wait to ____________ around Europe when I am older.

   a. travel   **b.** photographer **c.** exciting   **d.** trip

✔ Comprehension Check

Main Idea & Details

▶ **Read the sentences below. Choose the best answer.**

1. The article is about a(n) _____________ . **Main Idea**
   - **a.** traveling in Iraq
   - **b.** a trip to Asia
   - **c.** photographers
   - **d.** the Taj Mahal

2. Asia has the _____________ in the world. **Details**
   - **a.** largest area of land
   - **b.** second largest area of land
   - **c.** most different countries
   - **d.** smallest number of countries

3. The family traveled _____________ from Iraq to reach India. **Details**
   - **a.** northeast
   - **b.** south
   - **c.** east
   - **d.** southeast

Reading Comprehension

▶ **Circle T for true or F for false.**

1. A king built the Taj Mahal for his daughter after she died.   T   F

2. My family walked 6,000 km from China to Cambodia.   T   F

3. I learn about geography because I travel with my parents.   T   F

Focus on Skill

▶ **Look at the map to see where things are. Choose the correct answers.**

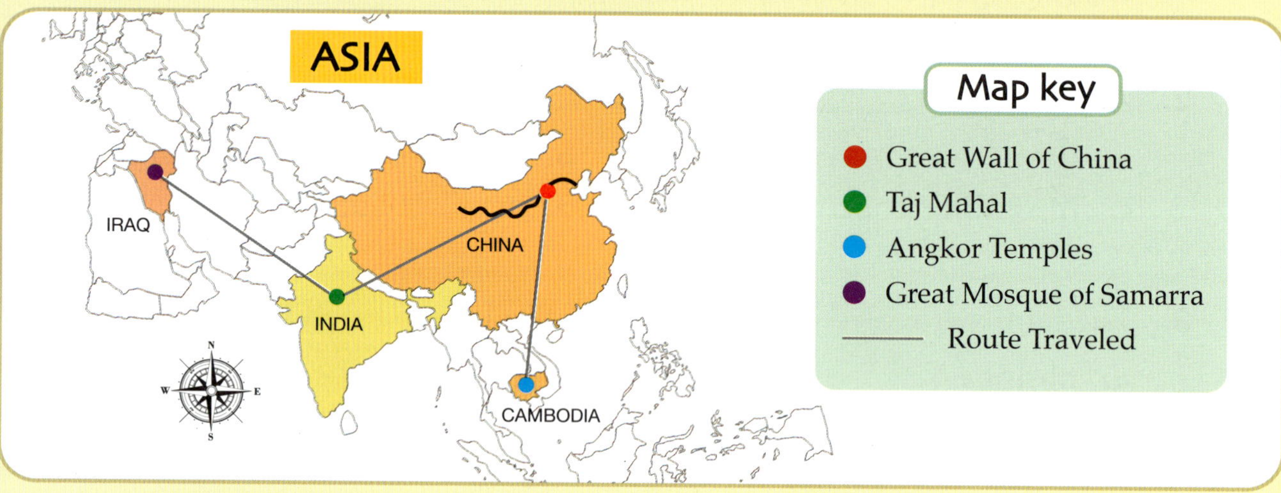

1. The Great Wall of China is to the ____________ of the Angkor Temples.

   a. north   **b.** west   **c.** south   **d.** east

2. The Great Mosque of Samarra is to the ____________ of the Great Wall of China.

   a. north   **b.** west   **c.** south   **d.** east

3. The ____________ are / is the farthest south on the map.

   a. Taj Mahal   **b.** Great Mosque of Samara
   c. Angkor Temples   **d.** Great Wall of China

4. The ____________ is in India.

   a. Taj Mahal   **b.** Great Mosque of Samara
   c. Angkor Temples   **d.** Great Wall of China

READING SKILL

Tables are a good way of comparing different things. Words and numbers can be organized in columns and rows.

Skill Strategy Read *rows* from left to right, and *columns* by looking up and down.

▶ **Read the story and fill in the table.**

John was making dinner for himself and six friends. He had $55 to spend on food. He wanted to buy seven steaks but they were $8 each. He did not have enough money! He bought 14 lamb chops for $2.50 each instead. Then he had enough money to buy seven baked potatoes for $1 each and seven cupcakes at $1.50. It was going to be a great dinner!

Type of food	Steak	Lamb chop	Baked potato	Cupcake
Number bought	0	**1.**	7	7
Cost each	**2.**	$2.50	$1	**3.**
Amount spent	$0	$35	**4.**	$10.50
Total spent	$52.50			

Before you read

1. Would you like to own a business?

2. What kind of store would you have?

VOCABULARY

stall n.
a small counter where things are shown for sale

business n.
the act of giving goods or help to get money

account n.
a record of the money that has been given out and taken in

check v.
to get information by looking at

check

Toy Stall

Steve owned a toy **stall**. His father owned it before him and his grandfather had owned it before that.

He loved seeing children playing with the things they bought. But the stall was his **business** so he had to make money too.

Every time he sold something, he wrote the information in an **accounts** book. Then he **checked** his **profit** at the end of the month. He **organized** the information in a table to see how much money he had made.

He bought **kites** for $3 and sold them for $6, so he made $3 from each sale. However, only 15 customers bought kites in July. He made $45 from selling them.

He bought soccer balls for $4 and sold them for $5. He only made a dollar for every soccer ball but in July he sold 50! He made $50 dollars.

soccer ball

Marbles also sold very well in his store. He sold 300 marbles this July alone! He bought them for 40 cents each but sold them for 80 cents each. So he made $120 from marbles even though he only got 40 cents each time.

marbles

He also had two bikes to sell at $90 each. He had paid $60 for each bike, so selling one would make him $30. However, he didn't sell any bikes this month.

kite

profit n.
the money made by a business

organize v.
to put things in order

kite n.
a toy that flies in the air on a string

marble n.
a little glass ball used in some children's games

bike

Fill in the Blank

▶ **Match each key word with its definition. Write the word in the blank.**

profit	marble	kite	account

1. a record of the money that has been given out and taken in __________

2. the money made by a business __________

3. a little glass ball used in some children's games __________

4. a toy that flies in the air on a string __________

Complete the Sentence

▶ **Choose the word that best completes the sentence.**

1. I had to __________ the meaning of the word in a dictionary.

   a. organize   **b.** imagine   **c.** check   **d.** guess

2. We sold lemonade at a __________ in our front yard.

   a. supermarket   **b.** shopping mall   **c.** stall   **d.** post office

3. My dad makes money from his pizza parlor. The restaurant is his __________.

   a. business   **b.** study   **c.** sport   **d.** loss

4. It is important to __________ your school books so that you don't lose them.

   a. inform   **b.** organize   **c.** throw   **d.** forget

Main Idea & Details

▶ **Read the sentences below. Choose the best answer.**

1. The article is about a(n) ______________ . *Main Idea*
   a. Steve°Øs business
   b. selling bikes
   c. buying marbles
   d. organizing information

2. Steve checked his profits at the end of every ______________ . *Details*
   a. day
   b. week
   c. month
   d. year

3. He sold the most ______________ in July. *Details*
   a. kites
   b. soccer balls
   c. marbles
   d. bikes

Reading Comprehension

▶ **Circle T for true or F for false.**

1. Steve sold kites for $5 each.   T   F

2. Steve's father owned the store before him.   T   F

3. Steve made a lot of money selling bikes in July. T   F

Focus on Skill

Using Tables

Tables are a good way of understanding and finding information. They can be organized in columns and rows. Rows go from left to right. Columns go up and down.

▶ **Look at the table showing what Steve sold. Fill in the table.**

Item	kite	soccer ball	marble	bike
Price bought for ($)	3.00	4.00	0.40	60.00
Price sold for ($)	**1.**	5.00	0.80	**2.**
Number sold for	15	50	300	**3.**
Profit ($)	45.00	**4.**	120.00	$52.50
Total profit ($)	215.00			

▶ **Choose the correct answer to complete each sentence.**

1. Steve made the most money selling ____________ .

   a. kites **b.** soccer balls **c.** marbles **d.** bikes

2. Steve made ____________ for every marble he sold.

   a. 40 dollars **b.** 40 cents **c.** 80 cents **d.** 30 dollars

3. Steve would make $0 profit by selling ____________ .

   a. kites **b.** soccer balls **c.** marbles **d.** bikes

4. Steve sold ____________ kites this month

   a. 15 **b.** 40 **c.** 200 **d.** 0

 # Using Graphs

> **READING SKILL**
>
> **Graphs** or charts are pictures that give information. They can make it easy to compare numbers.
>
> **Skill Strategy** When you read a passage, think about which numbers might be in the graph.

▶ **Look at the bar graph. Choose the correct answer.**

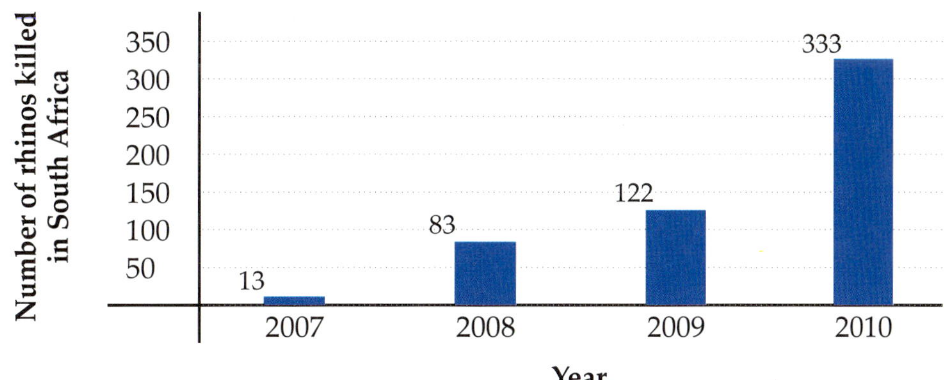

1. There were _______ rhinos killed in 2009.

    a. 13　　　　**b.** 83　　　　**c.** 122　　　　**d.** 333

2. In ___________, 83 rhinos were killed.

    a. 2007　　　　**b.** 2008　　　　**c.** 2009　　　　**d.** 2010

2. The most rhinos were killed in ___________.

    a. 2007　　　　**b.** 2008　　　　**c.** 2009　　　　**d.** 2010

Animals in Danger

Around 30,000 **species** go extinct in the world each year. Many are plants and insects, but some larger animals are also in danger of dying out.

There are thought to be around 3,200 tigers left in the **wild**. People **poach** the tigers to use their body parts in Chinese medicine. This and having their forests cut down has made them an **endangered** species.

Mountain gorillas are also endangered, with only about 800 left in the wild. Many of the African mountain forests they live in have been cut down for wood or damaged by **war**.

Also, there are only about 1,600 giant pandas left in the wild, living in mountain areas in Southwest China. Large areas of the bamboo forests that they live in have been cut down by people living nearby.

Another endangered animal is the Pacific leatherback turtle. It is the largest species of sea turtle and has been on Earth for more than a hundred million years. But now there are only around 2,300 left in the Pacific Ocean. Many are killed by fishing boats, and rising sea temperatures are also making it more difficult for them to **survive**.

Many **charities** are working to protect endangered animals like these. They try to protect their **habitats** so the animals can continue to live and grow.

Fill in the Blank

▶ **Match each key word with its definition. Write the word in the blank.**

poach	charity	species	wild

1. a natural state ________________

2. to catch or kill an animal illegally ________________

3. an organization that does good by helping people or animals in need ________________

4. a group of living things that are the same ________________

Complete the Sentence

▶ **Choose the word that best completes the sentence.**

1. The ocean is a shark's natural ________________.
  a. habitat   **b.** poison   **c.** problem   **d.** danger

2. We cannot ________________ without breathing air.
  a. smile   **b.** drink   **c.** survive   **d.** eat

3. When there are very few of an animal left in the wild, it is a(n) ________________ species.
  a. safe   **b.** numerous   **c.** endangered   **d.** common

4. The two countries have been fighting each other in a ________________.
  a. game   **b.** friendship   **c.** charity   **d.** war

Main Idea & Details

▶ **Read the sentences below. Choose the best answer.**

1. The story is about ______________ . *(Main Idea)*
   a. mountain gorillas
   b. Pacific leatherback turtles
   c. protecting habitats
   d. endangered species

2. Tigers are in danger from ______________ . *(Details)*
   a. being killed by war
   b. being poached for body parts
   c. rising sea temperatures
   d. losing their bamboo forests

3. Turtles are in danger from ______________ . *(Details)*
   a. losing their forests
   b. being killed by war
   c. fishing boats
   d. falling sea temperatures

Reading Comprehension

▶ **Circle T for true or F for false.**

1. Turtles have been on Earth for millions of years.　　T　F

2. Pandas live in African bamboo forests.　　T　F

3. Around 3,000 species go extinct each year.　　T　F

Focus on Skill

Using Graphs

A **bar graph**'s title and labels tell you about the information being given. Read the labels below each bar to see what is being compared. Read the label next to the numbers on the left to see what the graph is measuring.

▶ **Look at the bar graph below. Choose the correct answer to each question.**

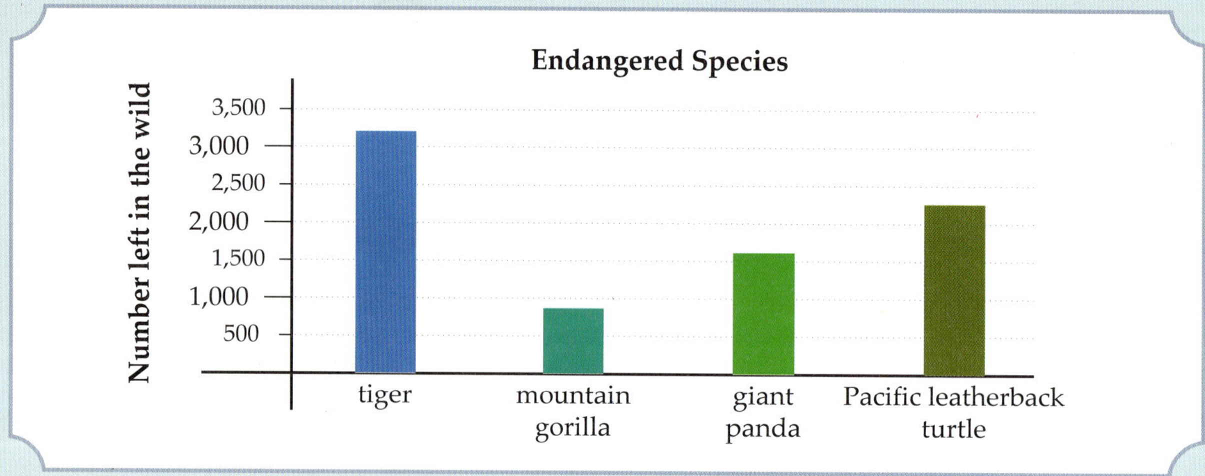

1. The animal on the graph with the least numbers still in the wild is the

_____________ .

   a. giant panda   **b.** tiger

   c. mountain gorilla   **d.** Pacific leatherback turtle

2. Out of the graph's animals there are the most _____________ left.

   a. giant pandas   **b.** tigers

   c. mountain gorillas   **d.** Pacific leatherback turtles

3. There are 2,300 _____________ left.

   a. giant pandas   **b.** tigers

   c. mountain gorillas   **d.** Pacific leatherback turtles